'As a functional medicine physician cancer. Mostly, I help them understa there and find resources to deal with i *Like a Lobster* is one of the books that the best explanations come from non-medical sources, and this is the case with this book. If you or a loved one is going through that journey, you will greatly benefit from this treasure trove of information to boost your mind, body and spirit.'
—Dr Alejandro Junger, MD

'A great practical toolkit for people living with chronic disease or those interested in understanding more about their bodies and pursuing longevity … A well-reasoned and researched guide to optimise your health using lifestyle measures.'
—Dr Mark Jinks, Medical Director, 199 Clinic

'A fantastic foray into the complex landscape patients are often faced with trying to untangle when dealing with a diagnosis such as cancer. At such an overwhelming crossroads in their lives it is often difficult to find a straightforward path to acquire the knowledge to understand and empower oneself with the tools important to try and combat this disease. With inspiration for change, this book is an essential read to help consolidate some basic tools that can be embraced and enacted in the comfort of one's home. The themes covered in this exciting body of work tie into the increasingly acknowledged metabolic approach to cancer and are a must-read for those faced with a diagnosis or recurrence of cancer. I applaud the structured and well-laid out approach detailed in the book in an easy-to-understand format, with some excellent examples echoed by many pioneers of the space.'
—Dr Hariharan Kuhan, Care Oncology Clinic

Published by Melbourne Books
Level 9, 100 Collins Street,
Melbourne, VIC 3000
Australia
www.melbournebooks.com.au
info@melbournebooks.com.au

Title: Live Like a Lobster: How to extend life,
avoid disease and confront cancer.
Author: Bridget Hancock BSc, Dip CNM, AFMCP
ISBN: 9781922779250
Cover design: Richard Harrington
Cover background image by Freepik

NATIONAL
LIBRARY
OF AUSTRALIA

A catalogue record for this
book is available from the
National Library of Australia

Printed in China

DISCLAIMER

This book is intended to supplement, not
replace, the advice of a trained professional.
If you suspect or know you have a problem
with your health, always consult a health
professional. The author and publisher
specifically disclaim any liability, loss, or risk,
personal or otherwise, that is incurred as a
consequence, directly or indirectly, of the
use and application of any of the contents
of this book.

Live Like a Lobster

How to extend life,
avoid disease and
confront cancer.

Bridget Hancock BSc, Dip CNM, AFMCP

M

MELBOURNE BOOKS

How would you like your life to look going forward?

To my precious children, Seb and Imi, fellow healers and all living beings, may you age gracefully, free of disease and live long, healthy lives.

Contents

Introduction

It was a sunny, brisk winter's afternoon at our stables when a good friend, Anthony, passed by on an afternoon walk with his family. As I led a young mare into the stable-yard, Anthony, a forty-year-old father of three boys under the age of twelve, stopped to tell us he had been diagnosed with cancer of the oesophagus. His eldest, he told me, had googled the disease and found out that he was likely to be fatherless in 9 months' time.

At the time I was training young horses, but my evenings were spent researching alternative cancer treatment. My mother-in-law was struggling with recurrent breast cancer and my husband had been diagnosed with bladder cancer. Now I was about to watch another friend battle with the illness and lose.

I had been interested in alternative treatments for a very long time, after my own experience of overcoming a life-compromising disease. Years earlier, I had been diagnosed with stage 3 kidney disease – a potentially life-threatening condition. With no advice other than to lose weight and not smoke (neither relevant to me at the time), I was told there was nothing I could do. I had to find my own solution – so I did. As a family, we adopted a more alkaline approach to our consumption – alkaline water, no caffeine or alcohol – and a much more plant-based diet. The results were astonishing – I recovered completely – and I developed a newfound understanding that we can change our health outcomes, which led me to take responsibility for my own and my family's health.

Even before my own medical issues, I had been interested in healthcare as far back as childhood, having had repeated brushes with illness and disease in those I loved. At age eleven, a good school friend was hospitalised, fighting a second round of leukaemia. When I visited her in hospital, she was blown up like a balloon on medication but after some time there and recuperating at home she recovered. It was the second time she had gone through treatment. Later, in my early teens, my neighbour and I ran around his family farm while his mother sat dying of cancer in the sitting room, strands of hair protruding from her otherwise bald skull. Perhaps as a result of these early experiences, my university years were spent studying drugs and their effects on the body – pharmacology and physiology.

Through my studies and my own brushes with disease, I had come to believe that, while of course genetics play a part in our health and well-being, what we expose ourselves to – including what we put into our body – can help to determine the course of our illness, as well as how to combat illness.

For the year Anthony was still with us, we had the daily pleasure of taking his three boys to school, helping where we could. But at night I would wake feeling powerless and sad. I knew Anthony couldn't rely on conventional medicine alone, but that was all he and his family were being offered to fight this terrible disease. A disease which I felt sure had been enabled by years of takeaway meals and gastric reflux, antacid medication and food choices, all of which had caused irritation to the cells of the oesophagus, leading to gastroesophageal reflux disease (GERD) and, tragically in this case, precancerous and ultimately cancerous cells. As I cast around for ways that I could do more to help Anthony and his family, I realised it was time to continue my education so I could share my knowledge with others suffering from disease, hoping I could provide tools to build their strength while they underwent treatment and maybe even help them achieve a better outcome.

About me

|

I am a naturopathic nutritionist with a BSc in Pharmacology and Physiology, and a transformational life coach with yoga and breathwork training.

My mission is to pass on to you the knowledge that I have acquired to transform and heal. To help you reclaim your health and support a life free of pain and disease.

I believe in our ability to reverse illness with diet and lifestyle. The connection between mind, body and spirit is a vital part of this healing journey. By simultaneously addressing the physical, mental and emotional states that lead to imbalances, deficiencies, toxins and stress, we can treat the underlying cause of ill health and begin to restore the body's health and well-being. And that is where I come in.

Now, what about you?

How did you arrive here?

Are you here because you've hit a roadblock with your health and wellness? Or have you sensed the gentle nudges your body is giving you, telling you something is up? You may be supporting a relative who is battling disease, or fear that their illness is genetic. Whatever the cause, somewhere in your life, an alarm bell has sounded, quite possibly very, very loudly. The body you've lived in and have been able to rely on is beginning to break down a little. For some of you, perhaps it has broken down a lot, and you're suffering from dis-ease – a lack of ease and a state where the physical body isn't working with its previous ease and well-being. You look back at your life and the years of making small decisions that seemed harmless at the time, but which have resulted in an accumulation of niggling issues. Maybe your stress and anxiety has risen to a level that makes ease of living no longer tenable – you're feeling highly strung, no longer able to cope with simple problems that once seemed to require little effort to handle. Or worse, you're coming to terms with your body's struggles and a disease diagnosis that means you need to make real and measurable changes to all aspects of your life. And quickly.

This book was written and designed as a support structure for those of you who want to take responsibility for your health. I have worked with scores of patients, many of whom are battling cancer. I see some people breeze through treatment and others struggle. I compare it to running a marathon. Even for the best runners it's never easy, but good preparation is key. The same is true for any age-related disease.

Whether you are struggling with a cancer diagnosis or noticing an age-related disease, you can make real and measurable changes at home. As you move through the following pages, you will find broad suggestions that you can apply to all aspects of your health and well-being, from the way you think about the food you cook and eat, to the holistic and ancient systems that support the nervous system. I treat the body as a whole vessel. All aspects of mind and body are connected. Nothing can replace seeing a professional for a tailored plan to suit your specific situation, but this book is a wonderful step to helping you along this journey. I invite you to make a shift to a lifestyle that will support your wellness and ensure you have the best chance of sustaining long-term changes to improve body, mind and soul.

Some concepts may sound daunting and scary, but this is information I wish I knew when I was unwell, and is the start of the journey to understanding and taking responsibility for your health and wellness.

Why we age

We are learning through science that the speed we age and meet death can be affected by how effectively we protect our DNA from damage.[1]

DNA is the material that is carried in our chromosomes and makes up our genes. It is unique to us. It is needed for us to grow, live and reproduce, and determines if our genes are turned on or off. Science is moving quickly, and over the last 10 years the field of neuroepigenetics – the study of the nervous system and changes to our DNA – has advanced.

The harm from stress, lifestyle, and exposure to toxins from the environment, our food and diet, and from household and skincare products all play a big part in determining just how long we live; they damage our genes and can switch on harmful genes and switch off protective genes.

A team of researchers at the Albert Einstein School of Medicine set up the Institute for Ageing. The team have determined that we have longevity genes, which help to repair the damage caused to DNA strands we associate with ageing.[2]

There are seven longevity genes which are responsible for producing anti-ageing proteins known as sirtuins, or SIRT for short. These proteins clean up damaged DNA strands and, in so doing, reverse some of the deterioration associated with ageing and disease. In other words, **we have an inbuilt protection mechanism to support longevity.** What we need to do is activate this and put it to work with various diet and lifestyle changes.

The second important factor in ageing involves the health of our mitochondria, the powerhouse of our cells.[3] Mitochondria create the energy in our cells to carry out all the functions needed for our survival. **When the DNA in our mitochondria gets damaged, they can add to the progression of cancer.** How we look after our cellular health will determine our resistance to disease.

In Dr David Sinclair's book *Lifespan: Why We Age – and Why We Don't Have To*, we learn that we can help to reverse the ageing process to support and activate the SIRT genes by changing our environment.[4]

Then there are telomeres, the little caps on the end of our DNA strands that act as guards for our genes. Our telomeres shorten over time and when they get too short, the cell dies.

Telomerase is an enzyme that lengthens telomeres, but is only present in sperm and egg cells. Why don't we make telomerase in every cell? If telomerase allow cells to divide then the absence of telomerase prevents uncontrolled cell division – a hallmark of cancer cells.

Instead we want to slow down the shortening of the telomeres and ageing by changing our diet and environment. Our chronological age (years) may progress, but our biological age (cellular age) can be slowed down, potentially keeping us free of age-related disease.

Lobsters produce the telomerase enzyme continually throughout their lives, protecting their DNA strands forever. In addition they live in extremely cold water where everything happens at a slower pace; their metabolism and heart rate are slower and like many cold-water animals, they live much longer than those living in warmer water. They also fast during the daylight hours, hunting for live food at mostly at night.[5] It has therefore often been posited that lobsters could potentially live indefinitely if left to their natural environment. Sadly we trap them for food, and lobsters go through the process of moulting which can leave them vulnerable to predators when their new shell is soft. Moulting aside, these cold-water animals have many ways to master their health. While we may not be able to stop the clock or live in cold water, we can adapt our lifestyle to make changes to our cellular health and therefore improve our health and life expectancy. We can lower our heart rate by exercising, reduce our stress levels with specific activities, and support healthy mitochondria by eating less often, all to extend a healthy lifespan. We can, in effect, learn to live like a lobster.

How do we do it?

We clean up our diet by removing sugar and starch and reducing our consumption of animal products. We make our exercise routine regular and challenging. We implement intermittent fasting, we allow ourselves to get hungry and comfortable in the cold, ultimately giving the body minor stress to wake the longevity genes. We lower our heart rate and learn to breathe more slowly and we use tools to reduce our stress hormones. These tools help us build resilience, maintain the health of our cells and lengthen our lifespan.

Doctors are essential

Doctors are trained to save lives. They attend countless hours in clinics, study for years, and shoulder relentless workloads and long hours. They need an immense amount of knowledge – that must be constantly updated – to treat each specific disease, and are themselves subject to rigorous scrutiny. Oncologists are continually working to find the best protocol for each particular case of cancer they are presented with. They are trying to kill a group of destructive cells that simply do not want to die. And with cancer, it is not a one-size-fits-all scenario.

But doctors are not focused on finding the root cause of disease. They are trying to keep you alive and work with broad spectrum success – and rightly so. Their decisions are not based on the latest media coverage of what food helps or heals. Unless it is a peer-reviewed meta-analysis (combining the results of multiple studies) with large-scale randomised controlled trials with proven success, they are quite correctly taught not to touch it.

However, when it comes to cancer and disease in general,

I expect all oncologists would agree that traditional medical treatment is better tolerated and supported by a healthy body.

What if we could support the body to heal itself as well as supporting the medication to speed up healing?

Just like looking after a car, if we add dirty fuel eventually it will not function properly. We can fix the car but if we keep putting in the dirty fuel we will continue to get the same results.

Why some smokers escape cancer

Much of this boils down to our ability to handle stress, detoxify everything that enters our body, and as a result we can manage the health of our genes.[6] If we look at cancer and disease as a result of stacking, then when stress is low, detoxification is high and harmful genes are not present to be activated. For this reason, it is possible that some people can live an unhealthy lifestyle without getting sick. If the brain and body are out of balance, this results in stress. When stress hormones are released, this can allow damage to our DNA, as well as lowering our immunity.[7] We can turn our genes on and off, so just because we have a harmful gene doesn't necessarily mean it will be active. Our thoughts alone can turn on our stress hormones, potentially making us sick. But what if we could reverse these thoughts to create positive emotions and make ourselves well? Take a look at how to turn off stress, page 147.

Can we heal?

There are countless cases of individuals reversing illness with diet and lifestyle changes. In Brandon Bays' book *The Journey: A Practical Guide to Healing your Life and Setting Yourself Free,* she shares her story of receiving a diagnosis of ovarian cancer, after discovering a basketball-size tumour stretching from her pelvic area to her ribcage, which was pressing on her diaphragm and causing internal bleeding.[8] She was told she could die within days. Brandon, a homoeopath, was horrified that she had failed her own health and asked her medical team for time to address the illness herself, rather than submit to the immediate surgery her doctors recommended the afternoon the tumour was found.

The book follows her journey until her medical check-up less than 2 months later, when the tumour was gone and medical intervention was no longer needed. This is proof that we can aim for optimal health just by giving our body the right environment to heal.

The right environment may differ to each and every one of us. But, fundamentally, we all need to consider everything we put in our body – from the air we breathe to the water we drink – as well as the environment around us, and to promote the daily removal of toxins from the body (take a look at Pillar 2 – Dumping the toxic load). We want to address our stress levels, using tools to lower them and restore balance to the body mind and soul (Pillar 3 – Stress: healing from within), and we want to include good quality nutritious food (Pillar 4 – The art of healing with nutrients).

My Story – Brandon Bays

I underwent radical changes in lifestyle, diet, exercise and my mind-set. Meditation, affirmations and visualisations became my best companions for healing. My day began with Pranayama, Yogasanas and Suryanamaskars. Silent nature walks, and a lot of self-introspection helped heal me further.

Homoeopathic medicines supported me to deal with the cancer and its mental and emotional effects. The ultimate healing factor was the unconditional love and support of my friends and family in The Journey, and my positive attitude to allow my body to heal itself … and to trust in its immense power of healing.

Lastly I allowed *love* and *peace* to be a part of me and stopped fighting with life. Instead, I accepted life the way it came.

Take a seat – How can I help you?

|

Let's start at the beginning. Let's look at how well your body functions – physically, mentally and emotionally. As a nutritionist and holistic practitioner, my job is to provide you with a framework to move gently but consistently towards a youthful vibrancy that helps you to get older without incurring an age-related disease.

In my clinic, I see clients in various stages of wellness and illness who arrive with a singular goal in mind. Most of my new clients are fearful and yet determined to turn around whatever illness or condition has brought them to my door. Many of those battling disease aren't sure they can rely on medical intervention alone to restore their health. Often they don't want to take medication, or perhaps they've tried treatment but it hasn't worked, so they have no choice but to address their diet. Almost always, they have previously been reliant on conventional medicine which can often provide a quick solution, but sometimes feels like a bandaid on a bullet hole. Perhaps medication has failed and they are left feeling helpless. However, the journey to the place where they now find themselves has taken years, often decades, to manifest. So making change – improving health and wellness – will also take time.

It is important to look at all aspects of self – the diet is key, of course, but lifestyle, emotional trauma, stress and previous illness all play a major part. So we start at the very beginning to see what has delivered you to where you are today.

At a consultation, we discuss your birth, the first 10 years of your life, your childhood accidents and illnesses, your primary caregivers, separations from primary caregivers, siblings, family dynamics, lifestyle, surroundings, school years, teenage accidents and illnesses, relationships at home and school, the health or demise of grandparents and parents. Thus, we get a picture of your overall start in life. Did you go to university, live in halls of residence, live with financial pressure, cook for yourself, party hard, get run down, negotiate illness, accidents, or addictions? How about your relationships, your career, work-life balance? Have you travelled to parts of the world where different bacteria reside in the drinking water? Areas such as Asia, South America or Africa? Are you self-employed? How do you cope with pressure and how do you relax? Have there been ongoing pressures in your adult life, financially or in your relationship, at the birth of a child or during their lives? We can put together a picture that provides us with the clues to where your body is struggling most, what is missing, and your levels of toxicity and stress.

Has your body given you any signs, whispers of illness or disease? When? Where?

Next we visit all the systems of your body: respiratory, digestive, endocrine, reproductive, musculoskeletal, nervous, circulatory and integumentary (skin, hair, nails and glands) by asking you a multitude of questions.[9] Some may seem relevant, others not, but gradually you may recall more and more events that have subtly and not-so-subtly impacted your life. The purpose is to create a mirror of your life that allows you to see how you arrived here.

How has your body been compromised by your journey thus far? Why is it time for change?

You can start this process for yourself at home by going through your life year by year.

Write a list of the answers to the enquiry into your life above. Add the major turning points: the game changers (large or small) that have had a behavioural impact; the things that have influenced the relationship you have with food and the decisions you make; the moments that have shaped your decision-making. When you have written the list, break it down into how you have responded to these life events. You can return to it later.

Once you see your life as a list in black and white, it becomes easier to map the journey to this moment in time.

What is wellness?

The Global Wellness Institute defines wellness as the active pursuit of activities, choices and lifestyles that lead to a state of holistic health.

We are exposed to toxins in the air we breathe, the water we drink, the food we eat, the creams we apply, our bath products, make-up, hair dye, tattoos, the carpets that help keep us warm and the sofas and mattresses that keep us comfortable.

Recent research has shown that babies are exposed to over 200 toxins via the placenta.[10]

But physical toxins aren't the only factor that affects our health. Your belief systems play a part: are you focusing on failure or what you don't have? This can affect your wellness and contribute to illness.

The positive effects of a healthy diet and lifestyle can be undone by stress alone, which can disrupt gut-brain communication, triggering pain and bloating and altering the gut microbiome. (More on gut health page 53.) This in turn can act on the bowel, causing diarrhoea or constipation and impact our ability to absorb nutrients. So even if we eat well, we may not absorb the nutrients to obtain the goodness.[11] In order to live with wellness, you cannot rely on healthy food alone; you must also pursue a healthy mindset and lower your cortisol; your stress hormones. (Take a look at page 144.)

Illness is defined as a disease or period of sickness affecting the body or mind. This can occur when viruses, bacteria or other microbes enter the body and multiply, or cells are not functioning correctly and the body cannot heal itself.

According to the Global Institute of Health, mental wellness is defined as an internal resource that helps us think, feel, connect and function; it is an active process that helps us to build resilience, grow and flourish.

Wellness is multidimensional

Physical: Nourishing a healthy body through exercise, nutrition and sleep.

Mental: Engaging with the world through learning, problem-solving and creativity.

Emotional: Being aware of, accepting and expressing our feelings and the feelings of others.

Spiritual: Inquiring into the meaning and higher purpose in human existence.

Social: Connecting and engaging with others and community.

Environmental: Fostering positive interrelationships between the health of the planet and our actions.[12]

The four pillars of health

|

Disease can be attributed to four fundamental factors:

Imbalance in the body

Toxic overload

Nutritional deficiencies

Stress

From this come the four pillars of health:

Restoring balance

Detoxification

Addressing deficiencies

Reducing stress

Your vitality, energy, focus, inner well-being, and confidence all depend on how well your body is functioning physically, mentally and emotionally.

Time for tea

|

I invite you to make yourself a healthy drink before you read on. Perhaps it's a squeeze of lemon in a cup of hot water, a hydrating and detoxifying drink, or you might want to try something that helps with digestion or sleep. Consider what life could look like if *you* take responsibility for your health.

The sole purpose of the cells in your body is to protect you and keep you free of disease so you can thrive. What you are about to read is designed to show you how you can help your body do its job.

Cumin, Coriander and Fennel Tea
Makes 3 cups

Ayurvedic detoxifying and rejuvenating tea. Ayurveda, an ancient system of holistic medicine, considers these spices to have therapeutic properties that support digestion, detoxification, and overall well-being.

1 tsp cumin seeds
1 tsp coriander seeds
1 tsp fennel seeds
6 cups filtered water

1. Pour 3 cups of water into a pan.
2. Add the seeds.
3. Add the remaining water and simmer until reduced to half the volume.
4. Strain and serve hot or, in warm weather, cold with a slice of ginger or lemon.

Ginger Tea
Makes 4 cups

Ginger contains bioactive compounds like gingerol, which have been shown to stimulate digestion by promoting the secretion of digestive enzymes. It is said to support liver function by increasing bile production, which aids in the breakdown and elimination of waste products. This is a wonderful anti-inflammatory tea, worth making ahead of time and taking with you wherever you go.

2 ½ cm piece of ginger root

1. Roughly chop the ginger to release goodness and place into a teapot or saucepan.
2. Cover with 4 cups of boiling water and leave to soak overnight.
3. Strain and gently reheat and drink warm or cold throughout the day.

Turmeric, Ginger and Lemon-aid
Makes 1 cup

Lemon is believed to promote liver health by encouraging the production of liver enzymes that participate in detoxification.

Juice of ½ squeezed lemon
½ tsp organic turmeric powder or half a chopped root
2 cm slice of ginger
Grind of pepper

Add to a cup of warm water and let it sit for 5–10 minutes, strain and enjoy.

Lemon Water
Makes 1 cup

Squeeze half a lemon divided into 2 large cups of water, enjoying the first on rising and the second cup before breakfast every morning to support the body's removal of waste by hydrating the digestive tract.

Drinking lemon juice in the morning has been shown to alter the microbiome (the microbes in our gut) to help improve digestion and reduce obesity.[13] Despite being acidic, lemon leaves an alkaline residue once metabolised and is great for balancing the bladder.

It is important not to have strong lemon water for fear of eroding tooth enamel. Only drink it in the morning and not throughout the day. Use warm not hot water to reduce the acidity and rinse your mouth with filtered water. Drink lemon water 30 minutes away from brushing teeth to protect soft enamel.

Dandelion Tea
Makes 1 cup

It's not by chance that dandelions thrive in the wild, readily available to us; nature often delivers an abundance of such medicinal gifts.

Dandelions contain potassium for cleansing. Potassium maintains fluid balance crucial for hydration and cell function. It supports kidney health, facilitating waste removal through urine, thus promoting effective detoxification.

Dandelion is great for digestion due to the bitter nature of the plant. Dandelion root encourages the production of bile, aiding digestion and liver function and so supporting the elimination of toxins. It also helps to regulate blood sugar.[14]

2 tbsp dried dandelion root

1. Cover the dandelion root with a cup of water, boil and allow to cool for 10 minutes.
2. Strain and drink.

Nettle Tea
Makes 4 cups

The stinging nettle, also growing wild, supports kidney function. It is rich in iron and minerals. The best time to harvest nettle leaves is in late spring or early summer. The leaves should be removed before the flower blossoms. taking just the top leaves from the plant.

A few nettle leaves from the top of the plant

1. Put the leaves in a pan with 4 cups of water.
2. Boil and then let sit for 5 minutes.
3. Strain and drink.

Rosemary Tea
Makes 4 cups

Rosemary is a rich source of antioxidants and anti-inflammatory compounds, which are thought to help boost the immune system and improve blood circulation. It is a stimulant, so should be avoided if you have high blood pressure.

If you pick fresh rosemary, dry the herbs for a few days somewhere warm before storing in an air-tight container.

Rosemary offers the mental alertness we get from coffee without the caffeine. However, like chilli, it can heat the body so may not suit some people.

2 tsp dried rosemary

Cover the rosemary with 4 cups of boiling water, leave for 10 minutes and drink hot or cold.

Lemon Verbena Tea
Makes 4 cups

Lemon verbena aids digestion after meals and can soothe period pains and cramps. It is also calming for the mind, relieving stress and anxiety.

3 large sprigs of lemon verbena

1. Place the lemon verbena in a teapot with 4 cups of boiling water and infuse for 5 minutes before drinking.
2. Serve cold with ice as a summer option.

Lobsters, like all animals when left in their own balanced environment, do not consume a diet of junk food and chemicals but instead live on a diet of fresh food. They can live over 100 years, grow to 5 feet in length and weigh up to 20 kilograms.

Pillar 1 – Restoring balance

A healthy body signals when to send in the army of rescue cells to repair, heal or kill, but an unhealthy body can trigger inflammation when there are no invaders to fight.

Inflammation

To restore balance to the body we need to promote physical, mental, and emotional well-being. We have to eat nutritious food, hydrate with clean water, allow time for repair with good quality sleep, exercise to support heart respiratory, skeletal and muscle health, spend time with family and friends, laugh and enjoy ourselves, but this alone is not enough.

We want to remove harmful toxins that we are exposed to daily and reduce the damage that stress causes in the body to make the body feel safe. When the body is out of balance, inflammation can appear and this is evidence that our diet and lifestyle may steadily be causing problems. Inflammation may not appear to have an effect on the outside, yet inside things may not be running so smoothly.

So what is inflammation?

Inflammation is a result of your body's white blood cells and immune system responding to an irritant.

The body signals when there is something wrong. The signal may appear as a rash or breakout on the skin, aching joints, gut issues, periodontal disease, digestive problems, fatigue, depression or insomnia. It may not be evident at all, as yet.

Inflammation occurs when your immune system – your own personal army – is activated to protect you against foreign invasion from an infection or injury. It is one of the most obvious signs that your body is fighting something. It is a quick response and switches off when it is no longer needed. However, ongoing inflammation – which does not switch off – can result in long-term damage and disease such as cancer, heart disease, diabetes, asthma and arthritis.

When your immune system attacks perfectly normal cells, this is known as 'auto-immune disease'. Let's address what inflammation may look like, whether we have it unknowingly and what to do about it.

Inflammation can be due to:
Poor diet
Infections
Poor dental health
Food allergies and sensitivities
Exposure to toxins
Poor detoxification
Obesity and insulin resistance
Chronic stress
Disrupted sleep

Inflammation:
Reduces immunity
Promotes tumour growth
Promotes metastasis of tumours
Supports new blood to tumour

Common auto-immune diseases include:

Irritable bowel disease (IBD)

Psoriasis

Hashimotos

Graves disease

Lupus

Multiple Sclerosis (MS)

Rheumatoid arthritis

Diabetes type 1

Do you have inflammation?

A blood test from your doctor can tell you if you have inflammation and is often part of a standard blood test.

Your doctor can perform tests that look for a marker known as C-reactive protein (CRP) to measure inflammation in the body. It is a measure of how quickly the liver is making this protein in response to inflammation or infection. A normal CRP level is less than 3 milligrams per litre. Ongoing raised levels of CRP are seen in chronic inflammatory conditions, infections and disease. A good example of ongoing raised inflammation is seen with rheumatoid arthritis.

Inflammation also leads to a high level of glycated haemoglobin, known as HbA1c. Measuring our HbA1c levels can help indicate if inflammation is causing our cells to become insulin-resistant. Insulin takes glucose from the blood, from the food we eat, to our cells to be used for energy.

When cells are insulin-resistant they fail to pick up the glucose and it remains in the blood, which causes damage to blood vessels leading to disease. Your HbA1c level should be less than 38 nmol/mol.

The erythrocyte sedimentation rate (ESR) test is a secondary measure to indicate the distance that red blood cells fall in our blood, due to gravity, over 1 hour. This is done in a test tube and the amount of plasma is measured after 1 hour. When inflammation is present, the cells drop to the bottom of the test tube very quickly as they clump together, making them heavier.

Inflammation is often related to our gut health.

Quick Tip

Signs of inflammation:

- CRP greater than 1 mg/dL or greater than 3 mg/L
- HbA1c more than 38 nmol/mol
- ESR over 30 mm per hour

How to lower inflammation

This is three-fold. We want to increase foods containing omega 3 fatty acids, add anti-inflammatory foods to the diet and remove the cause of inflammation.

There are two fatty acids that are extremely important when it comes to inflammation.

Omega 3 (ALA)
This is found in the chloroplasts of green leafy vegetables, as well as seeds of flax, chia, and walnuts. ALA converts into EPA (eicosapentaenoic acid) and DHA (docosahexaenoic acid) fatty acids, which are found in the oils of fatty fish, making these valuable additions to your diet.

Omega 6 (LA)
This occurs in the seeds of most plants (apart from cocoa, coconut and palm). It is present in the fats of grain-fed animals, dairy and eggs.

Over the past 10 years, in the western diet, levels of omega 6 have increased, while omega 3 levels have decreased. This is partly due to increasing amounts of processed foods, sugar, dairy, cooking oils, trans fats, alcohol, caffeine and meat in our diet.

As a result, the ratio of omega 6 to omega 3 has shifted from a healthy, balanced 1:1 to 20:1 or in many cases, 40:1, and this imbalance causes inflammation.

Research shows us that a diet high in omega 6 fatty acids can inhibit the anti-inflammatory effect of omega 3.[15] One key step towards lowering inflammation is to balance the ratio of omega 3 to omega 6 in your body. Adding omega 3 and consuming anti-inflammatory foods allows your body to correct itself when it is out of balance.

Extra virgin olive oil is great for salad dressing but contains omega 3 and 6. Flaxseed oil is more beneficial as it contains omega 3, making it especially helpful in avoiding or treating disease. Flax oil has the highest amount of omega 3 of all plant-based foods. We can use it alongside anti-inflammatory foods to correct inflammation and in turn slow down illness or disease taking hold. Flax oil is made from linseeds and needs to be stored in the freezer to keep it active. Flax oil comes to room temperature quite quickly and if you take it from the freezer when you start preparing a smoothie or salad, by the time you are ready to use it, you should have 1 or 2 tablespoons of liquid and the bottle can be returned to the freezer.

When it comes to cooking, it is high temperatures that damage oils. Olive oil for example, if heated, forms carcinogenic compounds, making it advisable to choose oils suited for high-heat cooking.

Avoid using highly processed seed oils, such as sunflower and rapeseed (commonly referred to as canola), as chemical compounds are introduced in the manufacturing process. The production of these oils typically involves methods like solvent extraction, bleaching, and deodorisation, which can result in chemical residues in our food and the creation of trans fats – inflammatory substances.

Consequently, opting for minimally processed natural cooking oils like coconut or avocado oil or ghee offers a more health-conscious and scientifically informed choice for culinary applications. That said, coconut oil has also been seen to raise triglycerides, which can increase our risk of heart disease, so ultimately, cooking without oils is the healthiest option. The introduction of air frying helps us avoid cooking with oils entirely.

Oils such as hemp, walnut, pumpkin, grape, or sesame seed oil add flavour when used cold on salads or after cooking.

Some anti-inflammatory ingredients to include regularly in your diet:
Berries

Cacao

Extra virgin olive oil: It's the least processed olive oil, although it does have omega 6 so may not alter the ratio, but a good fat regardless

Flax oil

Garlic

Ginger

Oily fish

Prune juice

Turmeric

Walnuts

Add omega 3-rich foods:

Algal oil

Anchovies

Chia seeds

Chlorella

Dulse

Flax oil

Flaxseeds

Herring

Kelp

Mackerel

Sardines

Spirulina

Walnuts

Wild salmon

Young soy beans (or Edamame).

Quick Tip

This is really the only fussy request made in this book. If you want to include flax oil into the diet, then ideally, decant it into small brown glass bottles to protect it from light and oxidation before placing them in the freezer. When you open a small bottle, only a small amount of flax oil will be exposed to the air. Packs of 5 x 200 millilitre brown bottles are available online.

The power of plants

|

Plants are extremely important when it comes to reducing inflammation. Without enough antioxidants we create zombie cells: these are cells that no longer operate as healthy cells but remain in the body causing havoc. They can be protective in our youth but as we get older they contribute to inflammation and need to be destroyed.

We can kill these cells with plant nutrients, known as phytonutrients. Some phytonutrients are known as senolytics. This means they can kill senesent (old and senile) cells – the zombie cells. These compounds, especially senolytics, are available in fruit, vegetables, spices, herbal teas and olive oil and can be added to the diet on a daily basis.

Quick Tip

Where to find phytonutrient to kill zombie cells:

- EGCG in green tea
- Curcumin in turmeric (not during chemotherapy)
- Fisotin in strawberries and cucumber
- Quercetin in apples and onions

Let's look at your gut

Looking after the gut can lower inflammation. The gut starts at the mouth and ends where the waste is excreted from the bowel. The small intestine is roughly 7 metres long but has an internal surface area of over 28 square-metres to maximise the absorption of nutrients through the walls into the blood.[16]

The wall or gut lining is one single layer of cells tightly packed together to prevent food particles, toxins and bacteria entering the bloodstream.[17] When the gut is compromised, rather than continuing the process of breaking down food for nutrients, absorbing water and sending the toxins to the liver to be neutralised ready for excretion, the tightly packed cells open and the contents leak into the bloodstream, causing inflammation and disease. This is known as leaky gut.

Leaky gut is a root cause of many illnesses, but is often seen in conjunction with auto-immune diseases. Inflammation is a driving force in auto-immune disease.

Studies show a correlation between leaky gut and lupus, multiple sclerosis and chronic fatigue. Leaky gut is associated with inflammatory bowel disease, irritable bowel syndrome, heart disease, obesity, type 1 diabetes, coeliac disease, alcoholic liver disease, non-alcoholic fatty liver disease, cirrhosis and collagen diseases.[17b] So healing the gut is the first step towards better health and reduced inflammation.

Do you have leaky gut?

After eating, I have gas and bloating   [   ]
I feel tired after eating   [   ]
I have had times of unexplained diarrhoea   [   ]
My bowel habits are inconsistent   [   ]
I am intolerant of many foods   [   ]
I drink coffee and get stomach pain   [   ]
After I eat, I have reflux or burning   [   ]

Although these symptoms may be a result of something else it is worth considering leaky gut. Leaky gut can be a result of antibiotics, gluten, sugars and unrefined carbohydrates (food made of white flour), stress, alcohol and medication such as Ibuprofen, all of which can create openings to allow undigested food, toxins and bacteria to leak out of the gut and into the bloodstream. Most of us, if not all of us have had our fair share of these foods and medications in our lifetime.

Bloating and reflux

Bloating after eating is a very common complaint and can often be dismissed as eating something bad. However, regular bloating after meals can be due to leaky gut causing food sensitivities and inflammatory reactions.

In your gut is your microbiome. It is made up of your gut bacteria, fungi and viruses necessary to supply nutrients, synthesise vitamin K, digest plant cellulose, regulate your immune system and support blood cell production.

The microbiome needs to be a healthy mix of good bacteria and these bacteria are easily destroyed by antibiotics, medication and a poor diet. If the microbiome is overrun by the bad bacteria, we get gut dysbiosis. This can cause bloating and discomfort. We need to rebalance the bacteria to support gut health. More about this on page 75.

In order to break down food, we need acidity in the stomach and digestive enzymes. Low acidity can cause indigestion, bloating and acid reflux. This is often incorrectly treated with antacids which lower it further, taking away the immediate pain but not solving the problem.

If you suffer from reflux, try having a tablespoon of apple cider vinegar diluted in a little water before you eat to build the stomach acid or try a small digestive salad before your meals (recipe on page 198).

If you find your symptoms improve then low stomach acid maybe your problem. If there is no improvement high stomach acid can be often addressed by a change in diet.

Low stomach acid can also result in a slower release of digestive enzymes to break down your food, and you may find a digestive enzyme supplement is useful here. Digestive enzymes are released when we smell food, making cooking and preparation of food important. Digestive enzymes also destroy any unwanted microorganisms in our food, protecting our gut. As we age our digestive enzymes reduce, so if digestion is slow a supplement maybe beneficial.

Bloating may also be the result of constipation, small intestinal bacterial overgrowth (SIBO), H Pylori (a bacterial infection in the linings of the stomach), Irritable Bowel Syndrome (IBS) or lactose intolerance. There are tests to take to determine if you have SIBO and H Pylori.

The test for SIBO is a breath test and, if positive, requires a rebalance of the gut bacteria through eliminating certain foods. It may also be linked to having low Thiamine, a B vitamin.

H Pylori is tested through a blood test. H Pylori is a nasty overgrowth that requires antibiotics and a gut healing protocol. If left untreated, it can lead to cancer.

Testing for food intolerance is not helpful when your gut is leaking, sensitive, over-reactive and driving inflammation. Healing the gut is the first step to managing food intolerances.

When we heal the gut, food intolerances often disappear, enabling you to eat a wider variety of foods.

There is no need to panic – bloating and reflux can signal the start of inflammation so needs to be addressed. Let's look at the 5 Rs to heal.

Quick Tip

Cancer patients benefit from pancreatic enzymes to break down cancer tumours as well as support the breakdown of food. Discuss with your nutritionist.

How to heal your gut

Change occurs when the pain of staying the same is greater than the pain of change.

Now you know that inflammation and leaky gut can be eliminated, you have the opportunity to heal your gut and change the course of your life. Nutritionists and functional medicine doctors may recommend the 5 Rs protocol. This is a process where you gradually build on the previous step to heal your gut.

The 5 Rs is not a one-size-fits-all approach. Healing the gut can take anywhere from 3 weeks to 3 months.

Patience is required:
Fighting SIBO, H Pylori, and parasites requires specific protocols. The FODMAP diet is one course of action and you need support from a nutritionist or functional medicine doctor who can establish the underlying cause, by testing, however this protocol is useful to us all:

Remove:
There are certain things that we need to take out of our diet in order to start the healing process. Ideally we want to remove all the offenders, including antibiotics, painkillers, gluten, dairy, refined carbohydrates and sugar. We want to stop feeding fungus, bad bacteria and parasites.

Removing stress may not be so easy to do, but I will show you ways to manage it.

Painkillers are difficult to remove if you are struggling with chronic pain so discussing alternatives with a doctor and nutritionist may be helpful.

Intestinal parasites are often picked up from contaminated food, surfaces, water, animals or poor hygiene. They can be responsible for abdominal pain, bloating and discomfort, diarrhoea, fatigue, nausea, vomiting or weight loss. A parasite mixture from a herbalist can help to eliminate parasites.

Replace:
You may want to take digestive enzyme supplements, as well as vitamins and minerals.

As discussed earlier, as we get older our stomach acid lowers; you may need apple cider vinegar to boost acid levels. Bile salts may benefit those who have had their gall bladder removed.

Reinnoculate:
We want to feed the good bacteria so they thrive.

Fermented foods are high in probiotics – the fermentation process contributes to the growth of these beneficial bacteria that support gut health. This includes kimchi (salted, fermented vegetables) or sauerkraut (raw fermented cabbage).

100 per cent full-leaf aloe vera juice is a nurturing but not particularly flavoursome drink and 100 ml taken morning and evening has been shown to support gut health, particularly through healing the gut lining and colon.

Onion, garlic, asparagus and green bananas are great prebiotics – foods that feed good bacteria. More to come on page 75.

Repair:
Supplements such as L-glutamine (not advisable for those with cancer or epilepsy), vitamin A, vitamin E, marshmallow root and zinc can support gut healing. Bone broth is also great for healing the gut.

Rebalance:
Eat and live mindfully, breathe consciously and take time to relax.

Note
–   *Avoid* self-prescribing supplements due to the potential dangers involved.
–   Vitamin A should only be supplemented as a retinol and *not* in beta carotene form, as it is dangerous for smokers or ex-smokers. Also, *all* forms of vitamin A supplementation are to be avoided during pregnancy.

Let's talk gluten

Gluten gets a lot of attention and we may think it isn't a problem, but do you get tired or bloated after eating? Even if you don't feel it affects you, it really does, so let's take it apart.

Gluten is a protein, one of many that we consume. It is found in bread (including rye and most sourdoughs), pasta, soy-sauce, couscous, bulgur wheat, sausages, sauces and gravies, thickeners, malt, processed foods, French fries (usually cooked in fryers that also cook gluten products), and breakfast cereals and oats that are prepared in a factory with products containing gluten.

Unlike other proteins we eat, we cannot completely break down gluten.[18]

Therefore it is treated like a foreign substance in our bodies, activating an immune response because we lack the enzyme to break it down completely. This can leave us feeling tired and bloated after meals. The truth is, for some people, consuming gluten may trigger a leaky gut.

Gluten-heavy, flour-based foods such as bread, cakes, pasta and pizza have relatively little nutritional value due to the processing of the grains. They are high in carbohydrates so best avoided if you are diagnosed with cancer or diabetes.[19]

Some older grains such as spelt may have more goodness, but still contain gluten which rapidly converts to sugar and is stored as fat.

Tiredness and bloating after a meal may not be due to overeating or eating too quickly, but can be symptomatic of the havoc that is going on inside. For those who are very sensitive to gluten, it can damage the intestines – this is known as coeliac disease. But even if we do not suffer from coeliac disease, gluten does not serve us.

Even gluten-free products can be problematic, as they generally contain additives, and create an unhealthy microbiome that can contribute to cancer and cardiovascular disease, so it is important that glutenous foods are replaced with fibre, fruits and vegetables.

If you go for a gluten alternative, it is important to check the ingredients to ensure the product is 'clean', meaning you can identify all the ingredients and make it in your own kitchen.

This doesn't mean giving up beloved dishes entirely. Innovative pasta alternatives like edamame fettuccine and lentil fusilli provide a higher protein content and are lower in carbohydrates than traditional pasta. Similarly, seed-based options can replace bread, as they provide superior nutritional value including more omega 3 fatty acids and essential nutrients.

Gluten Replacements:

Bread or Pitta: Replace with grain-free, spouted bread, Tahini Bread (see page 199) or Avocado Bread (see page 200), nori (seaweed) sheets for wraps; sweet potato, thinly sliced, is an unusual option for toast.

Crackers: Replace with Super Seed Crackers (see page 203) or Rosemary and Thyme Protein Crackers (see page 204).

Noodles: Soba noodles are made of buckwheat (always check the packet ingredients). Spiralised squash or courgette makes great spaghetti or noodles.

Pasta: Replace with clean pasta alternatives only made from edamame, lentils, soy beans, or black beans. Keep consumption to a minimum. Soy and edamame pastas are not for those with hormone-driven cancers.

Soy-sauce: Replace with Tamari (wheat-free soy-sauce).

Taco shells: Replace with lettuce or cabbage leaf to wrap ingredients.

Note
Soy is to be avoided with hormone-driven cancer.

What about dairy?

|

Almond, soy or coconut lattes are all very fashionable and perhaps you're already using these alternatives, but do you know why or if you are helping yourself?

Dairy also triggers inflammation:
Dairy may be responsible for congestion, the formation of mucus, or allergic reactions due to the proteins in cow's milk. This is particularly evident in singers who are known to avoid dairy before performances to maintain clear windpipes.

As a toddler, my daughter had a runny nose within minutes of drinking cow's milk, but as soon as she drank goat's milk it stopped immediately. It turns out she is lactose intolerant. Goat's and sheep's milk contain smaller fat globules than cow's milk so are easier to digest. Goat's milk is also lower in lactose, making it a suitable alternative for those who are lactose intolerant. Now we have goat's milk baby formula available.

In functional medicine (where we look at the body as a whole and look for the root cause of the problem) the first step in treating skin conditions such as acne or eczema is to remove dairy.

However, the reality is that all animal products present another concern: they contain IGF (insulin-like growth factor); a compound that helps the offspring of these animals stand immediately after birth and helps our bodies grow from childhood to adulthood.

As we cease growing, the levels of IGF naturally decrease. By the age of 55 years old our IGF is greatly diminished. It is no longer supporting bone density and brain health. Lower IGF levels are also linked to ageing and disease.

IGF has been shown to contribute to the growth of tumours.[20]

What are the best dairy-free alternatives?
Check ingredients of milk alternatives such as almond, hemp, cashew or coconut for additives, such as thickeners, stabilisers and sugar. Nut milks that do not have added rice or cereal are recommended in order to avoid carbohydrates that convert to sugars, raise glucose levels and store as fat.

In the UK, brands such as Rude Health (white carton only) and Plenish offer clean alternatives to dairy. In the USA try some of the Newbarn Organics milks; Australia, try Inside Out, but check the ingredients first.

If you are worried about your calcium, there are still plenty of ways to ensure you are getting enough calcium in your diet. Let's bust the calcium myth.

We all know calcium is needed for bones and teeth, and we have been taught in the west that a big glass of milk is the answer. In fact, too much calcium in the diet can cause calcium to sit in the bloodstream and harden in the arteries, a direct link to cardiovascular disease. Everything works in synergy, which is never more apparent than the relationship between calcium, vitamin D and vitamin K.

Vitamin D, from fatty fish, is needed for calcium absorption while also supporting the immune system, and vitamin K, from leafy green vegetables, stops calcium hardening in the arteries and directs it to where it is needed, in the bones and teeth.

A daily calcium intake of 1–1.2 grams is recommended.[21]

Where to get your calcium:

Almonds (10)	= 50 mg calcium
Blackberries (1 cup)	= 29 mg calcium
Brazil nuts (4)	= 25 mg calcium
Chia seeds (1 tbsp)	= 67 mg calcium
Chickpeas (1 cup cooked)	= 80 mg calcium
Chinese cabbage (1 cup cooked)	= 160 mg calcium
Collard greens (1 cup cooked)	= 266 mg calcium
Cooked chard or okra (1 cup)	= 100 mg calcium
Green beans (1 serving)	= 50 mg calcium
Green cabbage (1 serving)	= 50 mg calcium
Kale (1 cup cooked)	= 179 mg calcium
Kiwi (1 cup)	= 50 mg calcium
Onion (1 medium fried)	= 50 mg calcium
Pinto beans (1 cup cooked)	= 75 mg calcium
Red kidney beans (2 tsp cooked)	= 50 mg calcium
Rocket	= 125 mg calcium
Soy beans (½ cup cooked)	= 100 mg calcium
Soy milk (1 cup)	= 60 mg calcium
Spinach (1 cup cooked)	= 240 mg calcium
Steamed broccoli (1 cup cooked)	= 100 mg calcium
Tahini (1 heaped tsp)	= 66 mg calcium
Tomatoes (400 g)	= 50 mg calcium
Watercress (1 cup chopped)	= 40 mg calcium

Sugar is ageing

We all know that sugar is bad for our teeth, but it's also bad for our overall health, and more importantly, sugar is ageing. It affects brain function and memory, weakens the blood vessels, is linked to dementia, and causes our skin to stiffen and lose its elasticity.

In every form, whether it is refined sugar, sweeteners, syrups, honey, maple syrup, coconut sugar or agave – it's all sugar. As for stevia, it is not yet clear, as there have not been enough studies done, but studies show it may be detrimental to the beneficial bacteria in the gut and disrupt the balance of the gut microbiome.

As a healthy microbiome is essential to good health, it may be wise to avoid stevia.

Your pancreas releases insulin to pick up the sugar (glucose) from your blood and take it into the cells to use for energy. Constantly calling on the pancreas to do this puts the body under duress and can lead to insulin resistance, which is when the body doesn't respond, and leaves glucose in the blood. Equally too much insulin can result in the body storing fat which can lead to non-alcoholic fatty liver disease.

As mentioned previously, too much glucose in the blood can damage the blood vessels, increasing the risk of heart disease, stroke, kidney failure and problems with the nervous system.

Keeping your blood sugar balanced to avoid the rollercoaster of highs and lows is crucial in preventing or treating diseases such as cancer, heart disease, kidney disease and diabetes.[22] Blood glucose monitors, small patches that are easy to wear, can help you balance your blood glucose levels.

The use of the supplement Berberine after each meal can help take sugar into the cells to be used as energy rather than leaving it in the bloodstream where it can feed cancer cells.

According to a new study, a diet high in sugar is linked to Alzheimer's, giving it the title 'the third diabetes'. Sugar increases the production of beta amyloid plaque, the toxic plaque in the brain. It has been well known for a while that those with type 2 diabetes are more likely to get Alzheimer's, but this new paper released in May 2023 further reveals the danger of a diet high in sugar and the increased risk of dementia.[23]

Quick Tip

Try 3 days with no sugar, just enjoying vegetables (especially onion, garlic and asparagus), eggs, seeds, a little fruit, and an occasional serving of oily fish (salmon, mackerel, anchovies, sardines, herring) or 100 per cent grass-fed, pasture-raised meat to help rebalance your gut. As you build good bacteria, the sugar-loving bacteria in your gut go hungry, die and no longer control what you eat – and your cravings will diminish and eventually cease.

Cookies, cakes and caffeine

Some of our favourite foods such as chips, cookies and coffee contain high levels of acrylamide, a chemical formed when starchy foods are cooked at high temperatures.[24] Sadly acrylamide causes inflammation.

Cooking below 120°C stops the formation of this compound. It doesn't mean you can no longer enjoy some of these foods but it does mean you are better off making them yourself with healthy ingredients and cooking them at lower temperatures. Coffee is a little more tricky as it is already roasted. More about coffee on page 133.

Acrylamide is not just inflammatory. A study of over 120,000 people in the Netherlands over 16 years found that: 'acrylamide may increase the risk of cancer, specifically multiple myeloma and follicular lymphoma in men.' This is the first study to investigate the association between dietary acrylamide and the risk of lymphatic malignancies in a population, and more research is needed.[25]

Foods containing acrylamide:

Crisps	Crackers	Cookies/biscuits
Chips	Cakes	Coffee

The key to success

We all have good intentions when it comes to our health, and when it comes to New Year's resolutions, we make promises to ourselves to change. Unfortunately, these intentions rely solely upon our willpower.

Willpower is great, until we find ourselves under pressure. It works in direct competition with our dopamine pathway, which drives our desire to feel good and seek rewards. That sense of reward may be achieved by chocolate, sugar, alcohol, retail therapy, television, computer games, drugs or receiving affirmation on social media.

Have you ever wondered why a New Year's resolution doesn't last?
Willpower works until a trigger appears and the dopamine pathway takes over. This is the point when you might reach for a tub of ice-cream or a bar of chocolate, open a bottle of wine or buy something you can't afford online – and then condemn yourself for failing. At

this juncture, it's all too easy to give up and to struggle to start your regime again.

Companies have entire departments that work to lure you in and trigger your dopamine pathway, and it is very difficult to fight against this using willpower alone. This is where we need your gut to fight alongside your brain, to increase your chance of success. The key to success lies in identifying the triggers and healing your gut.

My Story – Chris Wark

Chris Wark was 26 when he was diagnosed with colon cancer. He didn't party or smoke and rarely drank. He lived on fast, processed junk food – a highly toxic diet combined with high levels of stress and negative emotions in his life.

In his book *Chris Beat Cancer: A comprehensive plan for healing naturally,* he shares the steps he took to heal himself using what he terms hardcore health advice.

– Christmas 2003. I was experiencing sharp and aching abdominal pain a few times per day, low energy, some rectal bleeding and dark stool. I was diagnosed with Stage IIIc colon cancer. There was a golf ball sized tumour in my large intestine, and the cancer had spread to my lymph nodes. I was 26 years old.

– I had surgery on December 30th, 2003, 18 cm of my ileum and colon was removed along with a golf ball sized tumour and 49 lymph nodes. Four lymph nodes tested positive for adenocarcinoma.

– I researched and found that the chemo recommended to me (5-FU-leucovorin) only increased 3-year overall survival by 4–6 per cent. So I decided against it and chose nutrition and natural therapies instead.

- I adopted a raw vegan diet beginning in January 2004 after reading *God's Way To Ultimate Health* by Michael Dye and George Malkmus.
- Upon rising I drank up to 500 millilitres of purified water.
- Then I juiced enough organic carrots, celery, beet and ginger to make 2 litres of juice, and I drank eight 250-millilitre servings throughout the day, nearly every day, for several years.
- Sometimes I ate a piece of fresh organic fruit mid-morning. Usually a green apple or a grapefruit.
- I ate a giant organic salad for lunch every day.
- I drank a coconut berry smoothie every afternoon.
- I ate super healthy nuts for snacks.
- I ate a giant salad again for dinner every day.
- Before bed I drank another 500 millilitres of purified water.
- I also did periodic juice fasts during this time.

After 90 days on the raw vegan diet, I was losing weight so I added 2–3 servings per week of either organic lamb or wild-caught Alaskan salmon and some cooked organic food like sweet potato, brown rice, lentils, quinoa, spinach, asparagus, squash, Brussels sprouts, etc.

For the next 2 years, my diet was consistently 70–80 per cent raw, and about 95–98 per cent plant-based. I kept it simple and basically ate the same thing every day with a little variation of cooked veggies at dinner and a serving of meat occasionally.

Fast forward to 2023. By the grace of God, I'm still cancer free, healthy and strong, and in the best shape of my life. I thank Him every day for my life, health and healing.

Prebiotics and probiotics

Probiotics provide us with our good bacteria and to multiply they require prebiotics. These bacteria, along with fungi and viruses, naturally live in our body and are known as our microbiome. Some are helpful and others potentially harmful.

Our gut bacteria play an important part in our microbiome as it appears they determine what we want to eat. The stronger the 'good' bacteria, the greater the desire to eat healthy foods.

There are many reasons why a healthy microbiome is essential. Some strains of good bacteria are responsible for producing many of our B vitamins, which protect us from viruses, and these bacteria are needed to absorb vitamins and minerals. Furthermore they break down fibre to form butyrate, which is an important requirement in our digestive tract. Butyrate is needed to absorb electrolytes, to hydrate our body, regulate our nerves and muscles, repair tissue and balance acidity. It has anti-cancer and anti-inflammatory properties and protects the health of the colon. We are often deficient in butyrate due to fibre-poor diets.

We need a diverse range of bacteria to promote a healthy microbiome, but the bacteria that feed on sugar are generally too well fed and thrive, taking control of our gut and driving our cravings for sweet things.

In order to have a healthy microbiome, we need to feed the bacteria different foods – time for prebiotics.

Prebiotics (generally carbohydrates) are foods that are not digested in the stomach, nor absorbed in the small intestine. They can be used alongside or instead of probiotics to keep the good bacteria alive, so they multiply and continue to reside in your gut.[26] If you are taking probiotics, you need to know how to get real benefits. In order to survive the journey from the mouth to the large intestine, probiotics need the support of prebiotics. On the journey they encounter many obstacles that threaten their survival, such as high stomach acid, temperature, bile, digestive enzymes, depleted nutrients and local bacteria.

Just like an army going to war without armour, they will be wiped out before they reach their destination.

The answer is to eat fibrous food within 30 minutes of taking probiotics to feed the bacteria to keep it alive, to lower the acid content of the stomach, and to support the bacteria on its journey to the intestines. If probiotics are taken with prebiotic foods, the probiotics provide food for the bacteria to multiply, giving them a better chance of making it to their final destination. Otherwise they die, wasting your time and money.

Prebiotics have shown to be effective in treating eczema and metabolic syndrome (a combination of diabetes, high blood pressure and obesity),[27] tightening a leaky gut, increasing insulin sensitivity and encouraging weight loss. Early trials indicate they may even prevent colon cancer.[28]

There are more bacteria than human cells in our body. In fact, our cells are outnumbered 10:1 by microbes, as noted in Alanna Collen's *10% Human: How your Body's Microbes Hold the key to Health and Happiness.*[29]

Probiotic supplements may not be advisable while undergoing traditional cancer treatment (chemotherapy and radiotherapy) as they can reduce neutrophils (a type of white blood cell) and increase your risk of infection. So it is important to discuss your diet with your oncologist or nutritionist and use a natural source of probiotic.

Top prebiotic foods for feeding healthy gut bacteria:

Artichoke	Leeks
Asparagus	Legumes
Barley	Linseed
Berries	Oats
Chicory	Onion
Garlic – cut and rest for 10 minutes before cooking	Tomatoes
	Unripe (green) bananas
Green vegetables	

Quick Tip

Jerusalem artichoke, roasted or boiled, is a great prebiotic to add to the diet to support a healthy microbiome.

Natural probiotics:

Fermented foods are a fantastic medicine. They improve digestion, reduce inflammation, regulate bowel movements, suppress the growth of undesirable yeast and bacteria, and are used in the gut healing protocol. In other words, they're great for you and should be a regular part of your diet.

Fermented vegetables, like those found in sauerkraut and kimchi, have strong gut-healing qualities and are incredibly beneficial for repopulating the gut with good bacteria, especially after antibiotics or any medications.

But not all fermented foods are created equal. Kombucha, although a good source of probiotics, is often manufactured with high sugar content and so best avoided unless you have a small local supplier and the sugar content is low. Be mindful of pickled vegetables as added sugar is often present.

Fermented foods:

Aged/raw cheeses	Pickles
Kimchi	Sauerkraut
Kombucha	Tempeh
Miso	Yoghurt
Natto	

Quick Tip

Other healthy fermented foods to consider include apple cider vinegar, sourdough bread, cottage cheese and coconut kefir.

The fibre pandemic

Many of us live on low fibre diets consisting of white flour foods and low vegetable intake. This results in sluggish bowels, which enables toxic waste to sit in the body, becoming stagnant and causing harm. This standard western diet tends to leave us eating less fibre than we need and cancers such as stomach, colorectal, pancreatic and even breast and endometrial are more likely with low fibre diets. It is a pandemic.

Fibre is a great source of probiotics. It nourishes beneficial gut bacteria, supporting digestion and immunity. Eating fibre supports the digestive process and is as fundamental as oil in a car.

Many of my clients come to me with a long history of constipation and with a change in diet start regular bowel movements in a matter of days.

Fibre is a type of carbohydrate found in plant-based foods that our bodies cannot fully digest or absorb. Its benefits are:

Promoting regular bowel movements: Reducing constipation and discomfort by speeding up transit time of waste and leading to regular bowel movements. This avoids exposing the colon lining to harmful toxins, thus minimising colorectal cancer.

Reducing stomach acid: Preventing irritation to the stomach lining and stomach cancer.

Stabilising blood sugar levels: Aiding diabetes management and reducing the risk of pancreatic cancer. Fibre-rich diets also lower LDL cholesterol, which reduces risk of heart disease.

Lowering oestrogen: Thus lowering the risk of breast and endometrial cancer.

The easiest way to increase fibre is to eat more vegetables. If you aren't used to having much fibre then build it up gradually so the digestive system isn't overwhelmed, increasing by 5 grams each day until you reach a daily amount of 21–25 grams for women and 30–38 grams for men.

Foods rich in fibre:

Acorn squash	1 cup, cooked, provides 9 g fibre
Almonds	95 g provides 11.6 g fibre
Artichoke	120 g provides 10.3 g fibre
Avocado	150 g provides 10 g fibre
Black beans	172 g provides 15 g fibre
Blackberries	144 g provides 7.6 g fibre
Broccoli	1 cup, cooked, provides 5 g fibre
Brussels sprouts	156 g provides 3.1 g fibre
Butternut squash	1 cup, cooked, provides 7 g fibre
Chia seeds	28 g provides 10.6 g fibre
Chickpeas	164 g provides 12.5 g fibre
Collard greens	1 cup, cooked, provides 8 g fibre
Flaxseeds	28 g provides 8 g fibre
Lima beans	1 cup provides 9 g fibre
Oranges	1 cup provides 4 g fibre
Peas	1 cup, cooked, provides 9 g fibre
Pumpkin seeds	28 g provides 5 g fibre
Quinoa	185 g provides 5.2 g fibre

Quick Tip

Garlic's effectiveness as both an anti-inflammatory and a prebiotic is attributed to its active compound, allicin. To preserve its potency during cooking, we can activate allicin by chopping or crushing the garlic and allowing it to sit for 10 minutes before cooking.

Earthing: An anti-inflammatory tool

Earthing is our electrical connection to the earth. It is used to restore our natural electrical balance to reduce stress and inflammation.

Once upon a time we walked barefoot and we were completely connected to the earth. With the introduction of shoes we have lost that connection. We also didn't have electrical devices and electromagnetic fields disrupting the millions of electrical communication pathways in the body needed for our health.

Without getting too deep into the science, the earth provides electrons that attach to free radicals in the body to make them stable. The free radicals are a group of atoms missing an electron and roam around causing havoc in our body. When they receive an electron, they become complete, no longer looking for trouble, and – just like anti-inflammatory foods – reduce inflammation.

Getting barefoot in nature, whether on grass, dirt or sand, for 20–30 minutes has been shown to reduce inflammation in the body.[30]

Simply touching the skin of someone who is barefoot on the earth can benefit you.

Earthing is also said to help to lower the effects of jet lag as it brings you into rhythm with the earth.

Quick Tip

Watch the earthing movie on Groundology.co.uk to see the effect of earthing on inflammation. For those who don't have time to get outdoors everyday it is possible to purchase grounding sheets for the bed and mats for under the desk to use in the home. They claim to have the same effect as being outdoors barefoot on the grass or earth.

Acid versus alkaline

*No disease, including cancer, can exist in
an alkaline environment.*

—Dr Otto Warburg

The Nobel Prize in Physiology and Medicine was given to Dr
Warburg in 1931 for his discovery of the nature and mode of action
of the respiratory enzyme. His paper written in 1928 established that
cells need oxygen to survive and that cancer cells live in low-oxygen
and acidic conditions and derive energy from sugars by fermenting
them the way yeast does. As cancer progresses, the body becomes
more acidic.

In 1966, at a lecture given to Nobel prize laureates,
Warburg said,

**Cancer, above all other diseases, has countless secondary
causes. But, even for cancer, there is only one prime cause.**

... the prime cause of cancer is the replacement of the respiration of oxygen in normal body cells by a fermentation of sugar. All normal body cells meet their energy needs by respiration of oxygen, whereas cancer cells meet their energy needs in great part by fermentation of glucose.[31]

Acidity is measured on a pH scale, 0 to 7 is acidic, 7 is neutral and 7 to 14 is alkaline. Your blood has a slightly alkaline pH of about 7.365. The pH scale is logarithmic. That means if a food has a pH of 6, it is 10 times more acidic than a pH of 7 (neutral). A pH of 5 is 100 times more acidic. The most acidic foods are soft drinks and especially cola-flavoured fizzy drinks with a pH of 3–4, which makes them up to 10,000 times more acidic than our blood. Meat, dairy, caffeine, alcohol, grains and sugar are also acidic.

Acid can be formed by a diet that is too high in protein, high levels of stress, or a lack of oxygen. Every day the body requires minerals to maintain the acid-alkaline balance, known as homeostasis. The pancreas secretes minerals to increase the pH to a more alkaline state. The lungs breathe faster to remove excess acid, and the kidneys produce bicarbonate to neutralise acid in the blood. If there is an excessively high acid load, or the lungs or kidneys are under-performing, then the body works hard to maintain this balance and may fail.

One theory states that minerals can be drawn from bones and muscles, resulting in osteoporosis (the breakdown of bones) and sarcopenia (the breakdown of muscle mass), and may potentially cause cancer.

If our kidneys and lungs are not functioning at optimal health they may struggle to support the process of maintaining the alkalinity of the blood.[32]

The power of vegetables may lie not just with the variety of micronutrients and the beneficial fibre to maintain daily bowel movements, but also the alkalinity they provide that supports the body to maintain an optimal environment.

List of alkaline-forming foods:

Vegetables:

Artichokes

Asparagus

Beetroot

Brussel sprouts

Cabbage

Capsicum/Pepper

Carrot

Cauliflower

Celery

Chives

Collard/Spring greens

Cucumber

Endive

Garlic

Ginger

Green beans

Kale

Leeks

Lettuce

Mustard greens

Okra

Onion

Parsley

Radish

Red onion

Rocket/Arugula

Spinach

Swede

Tomato

Watercress

Zucchini/Courgette

Fruits:

Avocado

Coconut

Grapefruit

Lemon

Lime

Rhubarb

Legumes and beans:

Buckwheat

Butter beans

Lentils

Peas

Soy beans

White haricot beans

Grains and seeds:

Quinoa

Spelt

Dairy and dairy alternatives:

Goat's milk

Tofu

Oils:

Avocado oil

Coconut oil

Flax oil

Udo's oil

Miscellaneous:

Most herbs and spices

Sea vegetables (kelp)

Sprouts (soy, alfalfa, etc.)

Quick Tip

Alkaline diets can improve magnesium intake, which supports vitamin D activation and are needed to boost immunity and support muscle and bone health.[33] An alkaline environment has also been shown to reduce muscle wasting.

Understanding cancer

Statistically, 1 in 2 people in the UK and 1 in 2 men and 1 in 3 women in the USA will develop cancer in their lifetimes.[34]

Yet evidence has shown that our genes account for less than 10 per cent of cancers.[35]

Cancer is an condition that I believe in many cases can be avoided. It is the second most common cause of death worldwide after heart disease.[36] Since the 1990s the highest growth in cancer in the UK has been in young people aged 0–24.[37]

In 2000 a list was established to confirm the characteristics and traits of cancer cells. This list is known as the hallmarks of cancer.

Ten hallmarks of cancer:[38]

1. Growth signal autonomy
Cancer cells can divide without the external signals normally required to stimulate division.

2. Insensitivity to growth inhibitory signals
Cancer cells are unaffected by external signals that inhibit division of normal cells.

3. Evasion of apoptosis
When excessive DNA damage and other abnormalities are detected, apoptosis (a type of programmed cell death) is induced in normal cells, but not in cancer cells.

4. Reproductive potential not limited by telomeres
Each division of a normal cell reduces the length of its telomeres. Normal cells arrest further division once telomeres reach a certain length. Cancer cells avoid this arrest and/or maintain the length of their telomeres.

5. Sustained angiogenesis
Most cancers require the growth of new blood vessels into the tumour. Normal angiogenesis is regulated by both inhibitory and stimulatory signals not required in cancer cells.

6. Tissue invasion and metastasis
Normal cells generally do not migrate (except in embryo development). Cancer cells invade other tissues including vital organs.

7. Deregulated metabolic pathways

Cancer cells use an abnormal metabolism to satisfy a high demand for energy and nutrients.

8. Evasion of the immune system

Cancer cells are able to evade the immune system.

9. Chromosomal instability

Severe chromosomal abnormalities are found in most cancers.

10. Inflammation

Local chronic inflammation is associated with many types of cancer.

Let's repair the damage

Understanding the fundamental characteristics of cancer gives us an advantage. We can change the terrain by implementing dietary changes, incorporating supplements, embracing detoxification methods, and adopting lifestyle modifications in order to promote our overall health.

When we dive deep into the imbalances in the body, the deficiencies, the toxic load and ongoing stress, we can see how our lifestyle may contribute to mutating and switching on destructive genes.

For example, we have 2 particular genes that protect us from cancer called BRCA 1 and 2, but if there are gene mutations (damage to the genetic code) they may no longer protect us if the need arises. This increases the risk of breast, ovarian and other cancers.[39] However even if we carry the damaged BRCA gene it doesn't necessarily express (switch on) and cause cancer – and choices we make can have an impact on this. Science shows us that poor dietary choices, lack of physical activity and weight gain can turn on this gene. However, there are also countless remission and recovery stories that occur simply by making big shifts in diet and lifestyle.

When we understand this, we can begin to actively pursue our own wellness journey. By providing ourselves with the right diet and the right environment, we can help the body keep destructive genes switched off and switch helpful genes on so the body can remain healthy or begin to heal itself.

With cancer we can try to repair damage to the body by:

Resolving infections
Removing fungus and viruses
Controlling inflammation
Reducing blood supplies to a tumour
Regulating blood sugar
Prevent metastasis
Improving detoxification
Supporting mitochondria in our cells
Reducing cellular stress
Increasing natural killer cells

Blue Zones

Let's take a look at the Blue Zones. The Blue Zones are 5 specific regions around the world where people consistently live longer, healthier lives than the global average. Generally in Blue Zones, 20–30 per cent of people live beyond 100 years, rather than the usual 2 or 3 per cent living to the age of 100 in the general population.

These areas, characterised by exceptional longevity and low rates of chronic diseases, were first studied by Dan Buettner, who identified several common lifestyle factors contributing to the longevity of these regions.

Three of the five are islands, the forth is a coastal region in Costa Rica and the fifth is in California – a religious community of 9000 Seventh-Day Adventists who are vegetarian, do not smoke or consume alcohol or fizzy drinks.

The 5 Blue Zones are:
Ikaria, Greece
Barbargia, Sardinia
Los Lomos, California
Okinawa, Japan
Nocoya, Costa Rica

In these regions meat is eaten sparingly with the diet made up of no more than 5 per cent meat and fish. In Ikaria meat and fish are enjoyed up to 5 times per month.

Could a diet based on a low amount of animal protein be a contributing factor in longevity and disease prevention?

The Japanese people of Okinawa eat a large amount of sweet potato (over 60 per cent of the diet). They only eat until they are 80 per cent full, known as Hara Hachi Bu. Finally, they fast overnight after the small meal until the following day.

What are the characteristics of Blue Zone populations?

In Blue Zones, people tend to follow a predominantly plant-based diet rich in fruits, vegetables, and legumes, with limited consumption of meat and processed foods.

A natural form of physical activity is an integral part of daily life. They engage in regular, low-intensity exercise, such as walking and gardening rather than time in the gym.

Social connections and strong community bonds play a crucial role in these areas, promoting emotional well-being and reducing stress.

Additionally, a sense of purpose and belonging, along with a focus on stress management and restful sleep, contribute to the overall longevity and quality of life observed in Blue Zones.

Protein

|

Protein calorie malnutrition is defined as a lack of adequate protein and calories in one's intake and leads to increases in mortality and surgical failure, reduced immunity, ineffective wound healing, poor response to chemotherapy and radiotherapy, and increased weakness and apathy.[40]

Protein is the most important component of our diet. It is required to build muscle that supports our skeleton and to keep our DNA functioning correctly. It maintains the health of our DNA and some proteins identify and repair the damage to the DNA that disrupts the genetic code. Keeping our DNA healthy is key to preventing disease.

Protein breaks down to amino acids that do the work, but we can't make all the amino acids ourselves so we have to get nine of them from our diet. These are known as the essential amino acids.

Protein comes in two forms: animal and plant based. Unfortunately most plant-based proteins are not complete proteins, which means they do not offer all the essential amino acids; or they do offer them all, but not at high enough levels. Therefore, we need to eat a variety of plant-based proteins to receive a complete array of all amino acids. For example, to build muscle we can eat pumpkin seeds for the amino acids – leucine, lysine and arginine – or combine pea and hemp protein. Animal protein provides us with all the essential amino acids we need, but bear in mind that meat and dairy are high in inflammatory omega 6. So, eating oily fish instead provides a good supply of the anti-inflammatory omega 3.

In our modern western world, red and white meat has become a staple protein. The average person consumes over 100 kilograms of meat a year which has increased by 20 kilograms per person since 1961.

When we consume animal protein, our healthy cells utilise the protein. In some cancers, amino acids from the protein such as glutamine can drive the cancer cells.

It appears that a diet lower in animal protein may be more beneficial to prevent feeding cancer cells.

In the 1960s scientist Dr T. Colin Campbell was working on an aid programme in the Philippines. He noticed an unusually large number of children being diagnosed with liver cancer. It was attributed to a fungus, aflatoxin, that had got into a peanut crop.

An interesting statistic emerged: although all the children who ate the peanuts were affected, it was predominately the children from wealthier families who died of liver cancer. When scientists looked further, the disadvantage to having more financial wealth meant these children also consumed a lot more animal products. The children from poorer families ate fewer animal products and relied more on rice and vegetables.

He came across a study in India in a small journal on cancer-prone rats that were given the same aflatoxins (a cancer-causing family of toxins produced by certain fungi).

A study fed one group 20 per cent animal protein and the other group 5 per cent for 100 weeks. All the rats fed 20 per cent animal protein died but not one rat on the low-animal-protein diet developed cancer.

Campbell repeated the study with similar results: after 100 weeks all the rats in the group fed 20 per cent protein were dead or dying of cancer. None of the rats fed the 5 per cent dairy protein had cancer.

Most importantly, when those with cancer had their diet changed from 20 per cent to 5 per cent animal products, all the cancers stopped growing and began to recede.[41] Plant-based protein did not cause cancer.

As a guideline, it may be beneficial to keep animal protein to 5 per cent of your diet: this equates to no more than 5 small handfuls of animal products per week. Lean towards good quality oily fish or high quality grass-fed and grass-finished meat in small quantities, on occasion.

Although fish is not everyone's favourite, it is important to include oily fish in the diet for the high omega 3, anti-inflammatory compounds. Aim for smaller fish that carry fewer toxins than those higher up the food chain. More on page 103.

Plant proteins such as hemp and pea protein, quinoa, pumpkin and chia seeds, walnuts, almonds, nut butters, greens and broccoli need to be combined but require consuming a greater volume to meet your amino acid requirements.

If you are vegan or vegetarian it's important to ensure you have complete protein which is not readily available from all plant protein, so consuming a variety of plants is important.

Try to use locally sourced food when you can as you will benefit by eating better quality meat in smaller quantities.

Grass-fed meat can only really apply to beef, lamb and goat, as chicken and pork require more than grass and so are often fed grain. It's worth noting that grass-fed can mean the animal lives indoors and is fed grass, which is not ideal. Pasture-fed means the animal roams the pasture and eats predominantly grass; however in the winter months in some countries, the animals may also require feeding; if there is snow-covered ground, these animals may also receive grain.

Plant-based protein quantities:

Almonds	16.5 g per ½ cup
Black beans	8 g per 100 g
Broccoli	4 g per stalk
Buckwheat	6 g per cup
Chickpeas	7.25 g per ½ cup
Chia seeds	2 g per tbsp
Edamame	8.5 g per ½ cup
Hemp powder	7.5 g per tbsp
Hemp seeds	5 g per tbsp
Lentils	8.8 g per ½ cup, cooked
Mushrooms	3 g (5 medium-sized mushrooms)
Pea protein	12.5 g per tbsp
Quinoa	8 g per cup
Walnuts	15 g per 100 g

Amino acid requirements for adults is met for all 9 essential amino acids in meat, fish and dairy.

Essential amino acids in animal proteins:
Histidine
Isoleucine
Leucine
Lysine
Methionine
Phenylalanine
Threonine
Tryptophan
Valine

Understanding the necessity to combine plant proteins for adequate amino acid levels using pea and hemp protein in a vegan diet.

Histidine
Present in both
Isoleucine
Low in pea and hemp need to add potato to the diet
Leucine
Not enough present in hemp
Lysine
Not enough present in hemp

Methionine

Not enough present in pea

Phenylalanine

Not present in hemp

Threonine

Present in both

Tryptophan

Needed from leafy greens, sunflower seeds, watercress, soy beans,*
pumpkin seeds, mushrooms, broccoli, and peas

Valine

Low in pea and hemp, need to add potato to the diet

*Not for hormone-driven cancers

**Eating your protein first slows down the sugars released into the
bloodstream from your food, preventing blood sugar spikes that
cause many age-related diseases.**

Staple sources of plant protein to add to meals to replace starchy carbohydrates or gluten:

Buckwheat: Despite its name, buckwheat is not related to wheat and is actually a seed. It's a complete protein and can be used in various dishes but is higher in carbohydrate so best kept to a minimum. Soba noodles are made of buckwheat but often mixed with wheat so check the ingredients.

Chia Seeds: Chia seeds are rich in omega 3 fatty acids and fibre and provide a complete source of protein.

Hemp Seeds: Hemp seeds are a good source of protein and are also rich in healthy fats and other nutrients but when added to the diet in powder form has 50 per cent more protein than the seeds.

Quinoa: Quinoa is a complete protein and a great source of various nutrients. It contains all nine essential amino acids, making it a valuable plant-based protein source. It needs washing and soaking for at least 2 hours prior to cooking.

Soy: Soy beans and soy products like tofu, tempeh, and edamame are complete proteins. They are rich in essential amino acids and offer a variety of health benefits. **They should not be consumed by those who have hormone-driven cancers.**

Malnutrition is a serious problem in cancer patients; anywhere from 40–80 per cent will be compromised.[42] 20 per cent of cancer patients die from malnutrition in the USA.[43]

How much protein do you need?

We also need amino acids to build collagen and contribute to organ function. Too much protein is stored as fat and too little keeps us hungry! When you have enough protein, your body feels content or satiated.

According to the World Health Organisation, the minimum amount of protein, so as not to get sick, is set at 0.83 grams of protein per 1 kilogram of body weight per day.[44]

This is the minimum not to be protein deficient, however minimum is not enough for optimum health and peak performance.

Your optimum amount is more likely to be 1–2 grams per kilogram. (If you are physically very active, it will be the higher end.)

If you weigh 60 kilograms you will need at least 1 gram x 60 (60 grams) of protein per day. You can get this throughout the day over 3 meals with 60 grams divided by 3 (20 grams).

It is not unrealistic for a physically active adult in optimum health to consume 1.5 grams of protein per kilogram of body weight a day. This drives the amount required up to 90 grams a day or 30 grams a meal or more. Protein intake doesn't need to be evenly spread out, and some meals may have more than others. What is important is that we add some protein to each meal to ensure we are satiated (feel full) and to preserve muscle mass and support our DNA. Some days it may be higher than others.[45] It is very easy when animal products are removed or reduced from our diet to forget your protein requirement.

As you now know, combining different protein sources can help you achieve all the amino acids you need, even if the individual sources are incomplete proteins.

Adding some animal protein, meat or fish to your diet may help to keep protein levels up.

I am not promoting the eating of animals. I am just providing information that may support your decisions when it comes to what you eat.

Research indicates that when livestock are eating a diverse array of plants on pasture, additional health-promoting phytonutrients become concentrated in their meat and milk.

Several studies have found increased antioxidant activity in meat and milk of grass-fed vs. grain-fed animals.

Small portions of animal protein can provide you with the complete amino acid profile require for optimal health.

Eggs: 2 provide 12 g protein
Feta cheese: 100 g provides 14 g protein
Halloumi cheese: 100 g provides 23 g protein
Meat: 113 g provides up to 24 g protein

More beneficial are these fish options that offer high omega 3 and are a great source of protein. We use the acronym SMASH as a great reminder.

Salmon (wild): 100 g (1 fillet) = 22 g protein
Mackerel: 100 g (1 large fillet) = 19 g protein and 89 mg calcium
Anchovies: 100 g (1 jar) = 29 g protein and 46 mg calcium
Sardines: 100 g (120 g per tin) = 19 g protein and 800 mg calcium
Herring: 100 g = 16 g protein and 105 mg calcium

Why organic?

Research from Harvard University shows that consuming fruits and vegetables with high levels of pesticide residues may lessen the benefits of fruit and vegetable consumption, including protection against cardiovascular disease and mortality.[46]

When it comes to detoxification we want to look firstly at the quality of the food we eat. The Environment Working Group (EWG) releases the 'Dirty Dozen' list of fresh produce annually to show those with the highest levels of pesticides and herbicides. Ideally only buy organic items from the 'Dirty Dozen' list. If you can't buy organic fruit and vegetables, wash them in 2 litres of water with 2 tablespoons of apple cider vinegar, leaving for 15 minutes to soak, and then scrub where possible.

The 'Clean 15' have the lowest chemicals and some have no trace at all and so can be eaten as non-organic.

Dirty Dozen:

Strawberries

Kale, collard and mustard greens

Nectarines

Apples

Grapes

Peaches

Cherries

Spinach

Pears

Bell and hot peppers

Blueberries

Green Beans

Clean 15:

Avocado

Sweetcorn

Pineapples

Onion

Papaya

Sweet peas (frozen)

Aubergine

Asparagus

Broccoli

Cabbage

Kiwi fruit

Cauliflower

Mushrooms

Honeydew melon

Sweet potato

Quick Tip

These lists are found online and updated each year at EWG.org.

A higher intake of high pesticide residue fruit and vegetables contributes to an increase in miscarriages. Replacing with organic fruit and vegetables 3 times a week has shown to lower the risk of loss of pregnancy and increase the success of fertilisation.[47]

Supplements

Remember: avoid self-prescribing supplements due to the potential dangers involved.

It's important to note that there isn't a universal guideline for everyone, and the quality and quantities of supplements can vary widely. Seeking guidance from a qualified nutritionist or functional medicine doctor is essential in this context.

Many supplements on the market contain additives and offer minimal nutritional value with little to no effect. Identifying trustworthy brands and determining the appropriate therapeutic doses of supplements requires significant time and effort, and is crucial in getting the effects demonstrated in research studies.

Avoid independently purchasing supplements, as this could potentially lead to unintended consequences. For instance, taking beta carotene might be risky for individuals who have a history of smoking, as it could increase the risk of lung cancer. Similarly, if your DNA type slows down the second stage of liver detoxification, taking vitamin C could speed up the first phase, keeping the contents of your liver in a more toxic state.

Due to changes in our genes some of us may need supplements in a certain form to be able to absorb them. For example, we may need to take certain B vitamins in a methylated form. Moreover, improper doses of supplements are a waste of money, so I strongly advise against supplements without obtaining sound advice from a knowledgeable source.

Vitamin C: Oncologists prefer it to not be taken alongside chemotherapy, but otherwise is best absorbed on an empty stomach before breakfast.

Vitamin D: Needs a fat to help absorb so eat with avocado, nuts, or olive oils and must be taken with Vitamin K.

Magnesium: Is best absorbed in the form of glycinate or biglycinate and taken after the evening meal.

Zinc picolinate: Is best taken at night away from magnesium to ensure it gets absorbed.

There are a few staples that most of us can benefit from such as …

Vitamin D3 and K2: Supports immunity, calcium absorption and bone health (but it must have K2 to take calcium to the bones, not the arteries).

Good-quality multivitamin: With cancer, ensure it does not have iron and for hormone-driven cancers try and avoid copper, and if it is difficult to do so add additional zinc to prevent absorption of copper.

Omega 3: Supports omega 3: omega 6 ratio to reduce inflammation.

Magnesium glycinate: Needed for over 300 processes including vitamin D uptake and relaxation.

Zinc picolinate: Supports immunity, makes proteins and DNA, as well as supporting our hair and skin.

Supplements for cancer need to be prescribed based on each specific case and individual requirements.

Keep coffee or caffeine at least an hour away from supplements so they aren't flushed out of the body rendering them useless.

My Story – Paul Reid

In 1997, Paul Reid faced a terminal cancer diagnosis. He was given 4–7 years due to a slow growing lymphoma. Seeking alternatives to conventional medicine that offered no solution in his case, he and his wife, Cheryl, embraced orthomolecular medicine, focusing on food as medicine. They revamped their lifestyle, addressing factors like toxins, dental health, and nutrition. Paul underwent a dietary overhaul at the Living Valley Spring retreat (QLD, Australia), emphasising fresh, plant-based foods. Cheryl transformed their diet, incorporating a balance of protein, fats, and carbohydrates using fresh fruit and vegetables, whole grains, nuts, seeds, culinary herbs, and spices.

Within 18 months, Paul achieved a clean bill of health, remaining cancer-free. Today, 27 years later, Paul is 82 years old and still cancer free.

*This is not for those who prefer the easy way out,
or for those who aren't prepared to rethink their eating habits.
It's not for the crowd followers, the conservative,
the faint hearted or unadventurous.*

—Cheryl Reid, The Healing Power of Food.

|

Lobsters graze at night, efficiently utilising oxygen and disposing of ammonia waste and using their antennae to find prey. Lobsters live in cold water, giving them the advantage of a lower heart rate and metabolism – fundamental tools for longevity.

|

Pillar 2 – Dumping the toxic load

The more nourishment you give to a person who has not been purged, the more harm you do.

—Hippocrates

Opening the exit

|

The road to health starts with your poop!

Before we cleanse, we need to make sure that your exit passage is clear. To be frank, you cannot be blocked up with poop! You need to be eliminating your waste once a day at the very least. Before you dump any toxins from your cells into your kidneys and liver to prepare it to exit your body, it is essential there is a clear passage.

When the passage of excretion is open, the liver and kidneys can do their work and remove waste. If the exit is not clear (for example, you don't excrete regularly or suffer from constipation), the toxins will recirculate around the body until they can leave. In the case of oestrogen, this becomes more toxic as it recirculates and can account for oestrogen-driven cancers.

In a healthy bowel, when enough waste presses on the walls this signals the time to release the waste. If you haven't consumed enough fibre then there won't be enough bulk to create this action. Eating white-flour foods does not support this elimination as well as fibre-rich options.

Quick Tip

- To keep your system working efficiently it can help to drink 500 millilitres of warm water with ½ to 1 squeezed lemon in the morning, but it is also essential to eat roughly 30 grams of fibre a day and include 6–8 glasses of water to stimulate waste removal.
- We can add herbs to the diet such as slippery elm and marshmallow root to support the lining of the gut passage and aid excretion.
- Psyllium husk swells to provide fibre: 1 tablespoon provides 5 grams of fibre but must be taken with water.

Toxins on our skin

Our skin is an organ that protects us from harm but it also absorbs everything it comes into contact with. This absorption depends on the area, the thickness of your skin, and its substance. The skin is a route for drug delivery via creams or patches.

Unfortunately, we can absorb less-welcome chemicals such as microplastics (plastic pieces smaller than 5 millimetres) from man-made coatings, such as paints, adhesives, plasters, polymers, cosmetics and personal care products.

According to the EWG, the average western woman uses about twelve products on her skin each day containing over 168 toxins.

Many toxins have been shown to have links to hormone disruption and issues with reproductive function.

Ways to detoxify your skin:

Activated charcoal: Can help to bind and draw dirt and oils out of the skin. Using it on the skin a couple of times a week can help with skin prone to breakouts.

Dry-brushing: Can slough off dead cells, increase circulation to support lymphatic drainage, and unclog pores.

Epsom salt: Baths also assist in detoxing the skin. Add a cup to a warm bath and rest for 20 minutes. Great before sleep.

Lymphatic massage: Can also stimulate the lymphatic system to keep it flowing. (Details on DIY lymphatic drainage on page 137.)

Rebounding: Jumping on a mini trampoline daily can keep the flow of the lymphatic system.

Sweating: Can improve detoxification of the skin, letting toxins out of the body.

Quick Tip

EWG.org or the Yuka app can tell you how clean your household and beauty products are. Using clean cosmetics and household cleaning products, eliminating or reducing the use of plastics, and attempting to use natural fibre bedding and unbleached cottons will all help to minimise the toxic load.

The air we breathe

At every cell in your body, specifically in the mitochondria, an exchange of gas takes place. Oxygen is exchanged for carbon dioxide – a waste gas which is carried in the blood back to the lungs, where it is removed from the blood and then breathed out.

For our cells to function well we need the membrane surrounding the cell to be soft and fluid to allow nutrients and gases to move in and waste and gases to move out.

Dehydration, low vitamins A, D, E and K – fat-soluble vitamins – low omega 3 foods and a poor diet can cause the cells to become stiff, making them less permeable so waste stores in the cells.

Let's look at how we breathe.

During a stressful situation our heart rate increases, which leads to an increase in short shallow breaths. The body relies on messages relayed by the vagus nerve, one of our body's most important highways which carries information back and forth mostly from the body to the brain. It controls the muscles in the throat necessary for speaking and swallowing, and carries information to regulate our heart rate and blood pressure, amongst many other things.

When we take shorter, shallow breaths, this prevents us from breathing fully to remove the unwanted toxins; our vagal tone is low which has an effect on our mental state and cognitive ability. You can test if your own breathing is shallow: if you put your hand on your belly and notice there isn't much movement in the belly, this is a sign of shallow breathing.

The key to fully expelling waste gas from your system is to inhale and exhale fully through your nose, as this tells the body it is not in a state of fight and flight. This can be accomplished with conscious breathing, bringing your awareness to your breath. By taking longer, slower breaths, you can move from shallow to deep breathing, which lowers stress hormones and helps to detoxify your body.

If you are lucky enough to live in a rural location, where fresh air is in greater abundance, I ask you to take some big, long, deep breaths through the nose, into the belly and exhale fully as part of your daily routine.

City dwellers can benefit from an air filter to help eliminate the toxic load you are inhaling on a daily basis from pollution. Just having fresh air overnight can help reduce the toxic load on the lungs.

Quick Tip

Air filters tend to operate using PECO or HEPA technology. HEPA removes at least 99.97 per cent of dust, pollen, mould, bacteria or airborne particles with a size of 0.3 microns (μm) or greater. PECO claims to remove pollutants as small as 0.1 μm, thus tackling the widest range of pollutants, including VOCs (volatile organic compounds) released from chemicals in carpets and furnishings, moulds, bacteria, viruses, and allergens. So either way either of these types of air filters are beneficial.

Hyperbaric Oxygen Therapy (HBOT)

Hyperbaric Oxygen Therapy (HBOT) involves breathing oxygen under pressure in a tank either sitting up or lying down. When we breathe, oxygen enters into our red blood cells. When it is pressurised, it also enters the plasma, thereby providing a greater amount of oxygen to cells. This offers additional support in taking oxygen *into* our cells and carbon dioxide or waste gasses *out* of our cells.

HBOT requires a minimum number of sessions to be effective: forty sessions for an hour (or an hour and a half in a soft chamber), 5 days a week for 8 weeks is recommended to treat cancer or disease. Soft chambers are often available to buy or rent but the Multiple Sclerosis Society is the most affordable option for those who can travel, with chambers available for a small fee.

Note

Using a hyperbaric chamber is not permitted if you have a history of pneumothorax, as it can lead to collapsed lungs.

The water we drink

Up to 60 per cent of the human adult body is water. You may live in a country where tap water is fit for drinking, but even 'clean' tap water is known to contain chlorine and oestrogen. Some of the cleanest and wealthiest countries have regions with high levels of oestrogen in the drinking water and in those areas there are high levels of breast cancer.[48] For this reason, it is safer to avoid drinking tap water, and yet it can be tricky to find an alternative. Bottled water presents its own issues (not least contributing to plastic pollution) – it leaks toxins known as BPAs and BPSs from the plastic into the water. BPAs and BPSs have been linked to increasing the risk of obesity, breast cancer and gestational diabetes (develops during pregnancy), and are toxic to the reproductive system.

Some plastic bottles are BPA- and BPS-proof, ensuring water is less toxic. Despite this, many bottled waters have depleted minerals.

A good-quality alkaline water jug that removes toxins (not necessarily oestrogen) as well as adding nutrients back into the water is a good solution.

A pinch of Himalayan salt is a quick, easy way to add minerals that have been lost through perspiration and long-term, gradual depletion of micronutrients.

In the long term, a mineralised water is ideal. Reverse osmosis water filters can remove hormones from water but also remove minerals, so purchase one with a remineraliser. Otherwise you can add mineral drops to ensure you get much-needed minerals back into your water.

Your thoughts

|

Western culture tends to celebrate life not in terms of our role within the community, or how present we can be in the moment, but rather in terms of our achievements and how we sit among our peers at various junctures. This view of life as a series of separate chapters is not unique to the west and has a very long history. As far back as the fifth century BC, in ancient Sanskrit texts, life was celebrated in four stages known as the Ashramas.

The first 25 years, known as Bramacharya, were about education, the development of the ego, and how we want to be seen in the world.

The next 25 years, known as Grihastha, highlighted the household, often time to settle down with a partner and make a family.

Age 50, the time for Vanaprashta, was when one might retreat to the forest and live life as a hermit, renouncing all physical, material and sexual pleasures. Going on pilgrimages, and giving back to community, devoting time to spiritual practice with others who sought solace and peace. These days, this stage may be interpreted as a time to retire. It may include travel, or time to enjoy the fruits of your endeavours, relax at home, enjoy grandchildren, or possibly navigate a new path, or serve others.

Finally, the fourth stage is Sannyasa, time devoted to spiritual growth. It seems that many of us shift our priorities the more time we spend on earth. Spending time with family and friends becomes more important than collecting material goods. This is especially apparent if we are faced with a life-threatening disease.

These later years are a time for growth and celebration. Children have grown, it's time to change pace and reflect on what life looks like.

When we arrive here we may ask ourselves, Is this what I expected or designed for myself, or did I get swept up, falling into something rather than engineering my chosen life?

Have you reached your full potential, achieved your life goals, followed your passion, and are you free to choose how you spend your days?

In our modern age, retiring is generally not possible at fifty and living in a forest is mostly not an option. However it is around this time that we undergo hormonal changes, and the consequences of a lifestyle choice may start to manifest as your body begins to show signs of malfunction.

To enjoy life, you require a healthy mind, body and spirit.

Life is about sharing with and serving others, whilst nurturing yourself in order to flourish. Connecting rather than consuming, having gratitude for each day, for ourselves and others. It's time to detox the mind.

Dentistry and heart health

Just a quick but important revelation about our teeth. Cleaning our teeth has more than just a positive effect on our oral hygiene. In fact the bacteria in the mouth has been found to transfer to the gut and has an influence over our gut bacteria. Inflammation of the gums is associated with inflammation in the body due to the movement of bacteria from the mouth to the gut.

The same type of bacteria that can be in the mouth has also been found in the heart, and is heavily linked as a potential driver of heart disease.

Keeping a diet clear of sugars and rich in plant foods, and flossing and brushing daily can prevent the transfer of oral bacteria to other parts of the body to protect the heart and gut health. It is suspected that bacteria travels from the mouth throughout the body triggering inflammation in the heart's vessels and infection in the heart valves.

Root canals are particularly of concern as dentists cannot guarantee removal of all infection in the root canal itself before it is sealed. The infection can manifest as inflammation and potentially disease in the body.

It appears that improving oral health can lengthen lifespan as we age, making regular check-ups and visits to a dental hygienist an important factor when it comes to heart and gut health and ultimately longevity.

Detoxing the liver

The liver is our gate keeper. It filters toxins out of the blood, neutralises toxins in the body to make them less dangerous, removes waste, breaks down fats in digestion and maintains healthy blood sugar levels by monitoring glucose supplies to the blood.

The liver processes poor-quality food containing pesticides, herbicides, microplastics, everyday pollution, chemicals and hormones in our drinking water as well as the chemicals in our carpets and sofas and skin products that are absorbed through the skin.

Once we have the exits open, detoxification of the liver is the next step to restoring health. It is something we generally neglect but need to address in order to keep it flushed and clean for the body to function well.

When we have regular bowel movements, we can start to pick up toxins (we call this 'binding') and take them to the liver for processing and elimination.

The process of liver detoxification has three phases. The first phase makes the food more toxic. We want to move waste along quickly to the second phase where toxins are neutralised. The third phase is the excretion of the waste created during the breakdown during phase two.

The best way to support liver health is with cruciferous vegetables; they are medicine for the liver. They contain sulforaphanes which support liver function. If possible, try to rotate the different vegetables for their added micronutrient benefits.

There is extensive evidence to show the benefits of cruciferous vegetables when it comes to cancer.

Studies at the Roswell Park Cancer Institute New York concluded that 3 servings of raw cruciferous vegetables a month reduces the risk of bladder cancer by 40 per cent.[49] Consuming raw cruciferous vegetables may also be associated with lower odds of stomach cancer, and people who ate more than 1½ servings of raw cruciferous vegetables a week showed 40 per cent lower odds of pancreatic cancer compared to those consuming less.

A study in the Netherlands on diet and cancer also concluded that 3 servings of cruciferous vegetables a week lowered the risk of developing colorectal cancers by 49 per cent.[50] The Fred Hutchinson Cancer Research Centre, Seattle concluded that 3 or more servings a week of cruciferous vegetables produced a 48 per cent lower risk of prostate cancer,[51] while a systematic review of 31 studies showed regular consumption of cruciferous vegetables lowered the risk of lung cancer by 23 per cent.[52]

Vitamin C supports the first phase of liver detoxification. To facilitate the swift transition of toxins into the second phase of detoxification, it's advisable to include cruciferous vegetables in your diet. Additionally, supplements like milk thistle, N-acetyl cysteine, alpha-lipoic acid, or selenium can be considered, although it is essential to consult with a nutritionist to determine which would be most beneficial for you.

Liver-loving cruciferous vegetables:

Bok choy	Kale
Broccoli	Kohlrabi
Broccoli sprouts	Mustard greens
Cauliflower	Radish
Chinese cabbage	Rocket
Collard	Turnip
Garden cress	Watercress
Horseradish	

Quick Tip

Include a handful of one or two of the cruciferous vegetables every other day into your diet, preferably raw or lightly steamed. Adding watercress to juices is a great way to get some cruciferous vegetables into your diet.

The magic ingredient for liver health is broccoli sprouts.

Broccoli sprouts are not to be confused with sprouted broccoli. Broccoli sprouts are grass-like and are great to add to salads or smoothies. These are 3–5 day old broccoli plants that are extremely high in sulforaphanes and the only food that really supports the completion of liver detoxification.

Simply ensuring they are present in your meals every second day can be hugely beneficial in supporting detoxification of your liver.

For those with cancer, 100 grams a day added to smoothies or salads is recommended. Broccoli sprouts are easy to grow at home – for information on how to do so, see page 276.

Kidney health

Our kidneys receive metabolites (produced from the breakdown of food and used for energy, cellular growth and repair) and filter them before eliminating the unwanted products into our urine.

Supporting our kidneys is paramount to our health. Eliminating the obvious culprits such as tobacco, alcohol and nicotine is key. Exercising daily and eating a healthy diet along with drinking filtered water is also important. Drinking mindfully means drinking a 250-millilitre glass of water an hour for 8–10 hours a day, rather than flooding the kidneys with the daily requirement taken all at once which can damage your kidneys.

Cleansing herbal teas made with nettle or herbs such as goldenrod, horsetail and corn silk help protect kidney function. Unsweetened cranberry juice is also beneficial to the health of the urinary tract.

The more animal protein the kidneys have to process, the harder they have to work. Reducing the intake of animal protein plays a vital role in promoting kidney health in those with compromised kidney function.

Maintaining a diet low in animal protein assists the kidneys in regulating the acid-alkaline balance, emphasising the importance of a predominantly plant-based diet. Recent research indicates a low-carb diet, high in plant protein and good fats, is key to restoring kidney function.

Coffee, the anti-nutrient

Just a note about our much-loved and relied-upon coffee, loved for its taste and stimulating effects and part of the culture and habits of people in many countries.

Coffee can increase heart rate and breathing, stimulates the large intestine, improves our energy levels and sharpens our mind, promoting a positive outlook. It may have a positive effect in protecting cells in Alzheimer's disease by preventing the build-up of amyloid plaque. However, more than 300 milligrams can cause restlessness, excitement, insomnia, nervousness, increased urination, disruption to the gut, irritability, and chaotic flow of thought and speech. (One black coffee is around 100 milligrams and remains in the blood for up to 9 hours.)

Caffeine causes a higher risk of inflammation in the intestine and stomach, and disturbs the uptake of some minerals including iron and zinc.

It has also been shown that more than 2 cups a day is considered toxic for the human body and can increase the risk of lung cancer.

Coffee is one of the most heavily sprayed crops in the world. It is sprayed with persistent organic pollutants (POPS) which are linked to cancer. Furthermore, POPS do not degrade and so are harmful to wildlife. Coffee often contains mycotoxins from mould. Some but not all of these toxins are destroyed in the roasting process. Mycotoxins are more likely to be present when beans are harvested and stored in warehouses where humidity rises above 12 per cent, allowing moisture in and creating an environment for mould to form.

Mould toxins can cause liver, kidney and brain damage, cancer, impaired immune and reproductive functions and gastrointestinal problems.

Coffee is also a diuretic (increases urine) so it encourages the body to excrete water more quickly, taking valuable nutrients with it.

For some people it causes a sense of urgency to empty the bowel. The colon is where water is absorbed, so your body loses water before it can be absorbed which can lead to dehydration and ageing. The kidneys are working hard and so when disease is present coffee is best avoided so the body is not constantly working and has time to heal. The colon gets time to rest, and the acidity of the coffee is not harming the walls of the digestive tract.

Coffee is a stimulant and a drug that would be best treated as a ritual. It can be beneficial when it comes to mood so if you feel you can't live without it, try keeping to only one small cup of organic coffee a day, to be consumed 1 to 2 hours away from any supplements in order to allow time for them to be absorbed and avoid them being flushed out due to the caffeine.

Although there are many good reasons to stop drinking coffee, it can be hard to quit. Coffee is highly addictive and can cause a headache on withdrawal.

I recommend removing it gradually to avoid thumping headaches. Try replacing coffee with 2 litres of filtered water every day or an alternative. Be sure to start the day with warm water and lemon to keep your bowels moving, and take a brisk 30-minute walk a day to help detoxification and minimise headaches.

Quick Tip

Replace your daily cup of coffee with one of these clean alternatives:

- Dandelion coffee with almond, hemp or oat milk
- Teeccino caffeine-free herbal coffee
- Rosemary tea
- Green tea
- Chicory coffee
- Lions mane mushroom, cinnamon and cacao blend that still contains a little caffeine in the cacao

If you still need your one coffee a day:

- Select high-quality coffee beans that are specialty grade and organically grown.
- Choose coffee that tests for the absence of aflatoxin and other harmful compounds.
- Try an Aero press to remove acidity from the beans.
- Select a brand that stores their coffee beans in a temperature-controlled storage facility.
- Choose a medium or dark roast that kills all mould.
- Choose Arabica rather than Robusta coffee. Robusta is a mono-crop meaning it is grown in large areas, causing deforestation and then eroding the nutrients of the soils. It also has more caffeine and is used in instant coffee.
- Choose washed beans.

Detox tools

Bathing: Adding half a cup of bicarb of soda to a hot bath and bathing for 30 minutes can help detoxify your body. Always take a large glass of water with you for hydration. Drink another glass of water after you bathe to flush out toxins. Epsom salt bathing will help infections and can reduce skin irritations.

Castor oil pack: A castor oil pack is used for a liver detox. It can be a messy process but involves simply pouring some castor oil on a light muslin cloth and placing it below the ribcage on the right hand side. Cover it with cling film and then place a hot water bottle on top to help to draw out the toxins. Keep on for a minimum of 2 hours, ideally 3 times a week, to help dilate the bile duct to release toxins. Ensure you drink plenty of water.

Lymphatic Drainage: The lymphatic system contains waste from our cells and, unlike the heart, doesn't have its own pump to keep the system moving. The easiest way to stimulate this system is to jump on a mini trampoline (rebounder). Buying a cheap mini trampoline and bouncing for 10 minutes in the morning and evening will get the lymphatic system flowing and is an effective detoxification tool. Start slowly and increase gradually up to 20 minutes a day

Manual clearance is also an effective way to supercharge the lymphatic system. Start left side first or both at once, just not the right side first.

- Stroke firmly down the side of the neck 5 times, then tap gently in the same area.
- Repeat for the clavicle area stroking and tapping down to the armpit.
- Then stroke and tap the centre of the stomach.
- Repeat on both sides of the groin, working downwards.
- Stroke and tap on the back of the knees.
- Then bounce on your toes, lifting the heels up and down.
- This will help drain the lymphatic system and shift your lymph containing toxins for excretion.

Enemas: Patients find this is one of the most helpful tools, as it can offer great relief to many patients on chemotherapy. Flushing out the colon gently with a coffee enema clears the system. It is said to open up the liver but the science behind it is a little unclear. The enemas flush out waste and potentially stimulate the liver to remove waste including the remnants of medicine once they have done their work to prevent it sitting in the body, which often causes nausea and more inflammation. What I can share is patients find getting the waste out relieves the side effects from medications sitting in the digestive tract being recirculated through the body. This is extremely helpful for those who struggle with constipation on chemotherapy.

A particular unroasted green coffee is used for its high concentration of palmitic acid, which is believed to support glutathione production in the liver which is required for detoxification. Additionally, unroasted coffee is thought to possess properties that can help stimulate the colon and promote bowel movements, aiding in the removal of waste and toxins from the digestive tract.

Enema Instructions

2 tbsp S.A. Wilson Coffee
1 L of filtered water
1 Enema Kit

1. Add 2 tbsp S.A. Wilson Coffee into a saucepan with 1 litre of filtered water.
2. Boil with the lid off for 10 minutes.
3. Turn down and simmer for 10 minutes.
4. Pour through a fine mesh sieve into a jug.
5. Top up to 1 L with filtered water.
6. Allow to cool to body temperature.
7. Lubricate the tube with aloe vera gel.
8. Put half (500 ml) of the coffee mixture in the enema pouch and let it run out through the end of the tube. Then shut it off, to avoid air bubbles.

9. Place a pillow on the floor, place an old towel alongside to lie on or use a puppy training sheet in case of leakage of liquid. Find a hook to hang the pouch so the tube is hanging down and when you insert the long tube (lubricated) via the rectum and open the tap and the coffee will flow inside. Hold if you can, up to 10 minutes.

10. Sit on the loo and let it go.

11. Now place ¼ tsp bifida bacteria in the base of the enema bag.

12. Fill the bag with the rest of the coffee mixture and proceed as for the first insertion.

13. Hold for as long as you can and release.

14. Wash the enema bag out with near-boiling water and rinse the tube with boiling water and store.

Lobsters use serotonin to govern their emotional regulation and posture just like we do. Just as we stand up straight with our shoulders back or choose to slouch in a depressed crouched-over posture, lobsters also use serotonin to support their posture. It is hypothesised that the more dominant a lobster is, the more serotonin is present in their body. Serotonin is the feel-good chemical that helps us with our muscles, movement and digestion while supporting our mood and a positive outlook for a long healthy life.

Pillar 3 – Stress: healing from within

He, who has a why to live for, can bear almost any how.

—*Friedrich Nietzsche*

Too much stress kills

Our ancestors encountered stress when they were chased by a predator or couldn't find food. We may not encounter tigers in our modern-day lives, but we have our equivalents. There are infinite modern-day stresses such as finances, traffic jams, social media, doom scrolling, climate anxiety, work pressures, or even caffeine.

When the body and brain are out of balance we release stress hormones that can wreak havoc with our genes and our immunity and don't switch off by themselves. Reducing stress hormones is a process that requires you to actively switch them off. Part of stress reduction may require you to alter your thoughts from a negative mindset to a positive, loving state.

The nervous system has two branches:
The **Sympathetic** (fight-or-flight) system prepares the body to muster up energy in emergencies or stressful situations. It releases adrenaline and cortisol into your system, to ensure you are alert

and ready to flee danger. The hormones cause the body to increase the heart rate, dilate the pupils, increase blood flow and at the same time slow down digestion in preparation to run.

The **Parasympathetic** system promotes rest and digestion. It is designed to support healing and repair, assimilating (absorbing) nutrients for use and excreting waste. Digestion and waste excretion for example are not useful when we are being chased by a tiger! It is, however, this branch we wish to activate at the start of our day when cortisol is naturally high and after a stressful day or a difficult conversation to bring it from flight and fight to rest and digest.

Research has identified three factors that universally lead to stress – uncertainty, loss of control and lack of information.[53] If you can step away from the cause of stress, you may think that is the solution, but in fact it is only part of it. This does not switch off your stress response. In situations of short-term stress, cortisol can stay elevated for 3 to 4 hours following a stressful event.[54] Prolonged stress causes cortisol levels to remain elevated for a long period of time – potentially 6 months or more. This chronic exposure to stress has many detrimental effects. Recent studies found a link between stress, tumour development and suppression of natural killer (NK) cells, which are involved in preventing metastasis and destroying small metastases.[55]

Eating while stressed is not good for digestion. In order to shift to the 'rest and digest' path of your nervous system, to support digestion and get the most from the nutrients we eat, we need to pause, to breathe well and to take our time.

The risk of ongoing stress:

Asthma attacks

Decreasing immunity

Diabetes

Hair loss

Plaque in arteries, heart attack and stroke

Psychiatric illness

Stomach ulcers

Tumour development and growth, by lowering immune cells needed to stop metastasis

Ulcerative colitis

VEGF, a growth factor that encourages blood to feed a tumour (more on this in the next chapter, see page 168)

Viral infection

Weight gain

Stress reduces:

Memory

Concentration

Sleep

Libido

Stress and immunity

When we experience stress our immune system is under threat. The sympathetic fight-or-flight arm of our nervous system is activated and our energy is diverted to where it is needed – the tools to run. We stop digesting food, our pupils dilate, our heart rate increases and our immune system is abandoned at this time and therefore compromised.

Firstly it helps to understand that your immune system relies on natural killer cells (NK) to destroy unwanted cells. These are a type of immune cell that are part of our early defence program, that defend us against foreign cells, infection cells, or tumour cells. Boosting the function of natural killer cells is essential to help prevent cancer.

We can boost these cells by stress reduction techniques such as:

Breathing: Using the full capacity of our lungs and our ability to breathe through our nose.

Exercise: This balances insulin and increases NK cell activity.

Massage: This increases the feel-good hormone dopamine and NK cells.

Meditation: This increases the activity of NK cells, reduces the stress hormone cortisol and reduces inflammatory responses.

Mushrooms: Button mushrooms or shiitake mushrooms boost the activity of NK cells.

Activities such as dance, music, art therapy, journaling, yoga, qi gong, tai chi, walking in nature, eating well, and getting a good night's sleep can have a positive impact on lowering our stress and promoting feel-good hormones.

How to switch off stress

Chronic stress can impact telomere length. Engaging in stress-reducing practices such as mindfulness, meditation, yoga, deep breathing exercises, and spending time in nature may help manage stress and potentially support telomere health.

Most of us are not using our full lung capacity to breathe, and we tend to breathe only into the upper area of our lungs. This is known as shallow breathing.

Recent studies have shown that just 5 minutes of cyclical breathwork reduces stress and improves mood. Breathing is an automatic process we rarely think about, but if we draw our attention to the breath we start to take bigger, deeper breaths. This awareness of the breath is known as conscious breathing, and is a very powerful tool.

By becoming more conscious of our breathing, we can reduce our stress hormones as we shift from fight and flight to rest and digest. A deeper, slower breath, filling the belly and expanding the rib cage to fill the lungs followed by a long slow exhale, signals to the body you are safe and you can switch off adrenaline and cortisol.

1-minute stress reduction technique: Conscious breathing through the nose helps to reduce stress. Try taking a slow inhale for a count to 5 and exhale through the nose for an even slower count to 5. Repeat 6 times. If you can extend the exhale through the nose for longer than the inhale, it will shift you into the 'rest and digest', the parasympathetic nervous system. It is a challenge to see how long you can exhale for, pulling the belly button to the spine to remove all the stale air before returning to a slow inhale.

10–20 minute technique: Meditation is also a key practice in reducing stress hormones. Switching off the mind and sitting still, removing all forms of stimulation, helps bring us back to the rested state. Try Soulsync meditation on YouTube for a great introduction to easy meditation.

20–60 minute technique: Traditional yoga, the unity of breath and movement, the practice of Qi gong or Tai chi allows us to switch over to the path of the parasympathetic nervous system. Alternatively, art therapy has been shown to increase dopamine levels and reduce stress, depression and anxiety with the added bonus of improving memory.

1–2 hour technique: A 2-hour walk in nature, investigating what you see, hear, smell or breathe is known in Japan as 'forest bathing'. Originally a stress therapy for Japanese employees, it has been shown to reduce stress, improve mood, boost immunity and lower blood pressure.

The breath

The 4–7–8 breath:

Dr Andrew Weil developed this breathing technique as a natural tranquilliser for the nervous system.[56] The longer exhale creates a nervous impulse to be sent up the vagus nerve to the brain, telling the brain to shift from fight and flight to rest and digest.

Sit comfortably with your back upright.

Exhale everything from the body through the mouth, pulling the belly button back to the spine to fully empty the lungs.

Inhale through the nose for a count of 4.

Hold the breath for a count of 7.

Exhale for a count of 8. Repeat 4 times.

Start small. Introducing a new activity with the least amount of disruption means you are more likely to stick to it. Attach it to a routine you already have – perhaps a 1-minute stress reduction breathwork before each meal, in bed or before a challenging phone call.

Get moving

|

Balanced exercise promotes good health. Excessive exercise, such as regular high cardio routines, can often make matters worse, driving stress and acidity in the body. Science has found that adopting a more gentle approach to exercise can help reduce the very thing that may be causing us damage.

Recent studies have proven the importance of taking 150 minutes a week of walking, or 75 minutes of more intensive movement. Ideally, a 30-minute brisk walk, 5 days a week, preferably before breakfast has shown to improve treatment outcomes for cancer.

Exercise releases neurotransmitters to promote mental clarity and improved attention span. We want to keep digestion moving and gentle exercise does just this.

By exercising daily, you are metabolising your food and excreting waste on a regular basis. If you are well enough, a short sharp burst of cardio activity is good for body strengthening and overall health.

If you are someone who struggles to exercise and it is not part of your routine, (only if you are well enough and not in pain), perhaps consider making yourself a 10–15 minute HIIT (high intensity interval training) class to do yourself.

Research has shown HIIT can help maintain muscle mass, support insulin sensitivity to support levels of blood sugar, bone strength, enhance mitochondrial function to maintain health and may help protect telomeres to slow down ageing.

Your personal HIIT program may run for 15 minutes. Pick 5 exercises, do each one for 45 seconds, with a recovery period of 15 seconds in between each exercise and repeat each set of 5 exercises 3 times.

A routine may include any movement that works for you. More intensive exercise options are lunges, squats, hanging from a bar with your shoulder blades sliding down your back, mountain climbers, star jumps or skipping with a rope – each one for 45 seconds with a 15-second break – for 3 rounds.

Releasing trauma

|

Take a deep dive into your heart: There are techniques to take thoughts, emotions or even trauma out of the mind and release the fear, pain or anxiety held in our cells.

A good practice is to notice what emotion you are feeling, and then try to feel where it sits in your body. Perhaps it manifests as a fluttering or butterflies in the gut, or tension in the neck. Feel it and ask yourself, What do I need right now?

Journaling: This practice may be new to you but at the end of the day it is effective at relieving stress and supporting sleep. Write whatever comes to mind – your worries or fears, your day gone by or what's planned for the day ahead. It is always good to end it with what has made today great or ask yourself, What am I grateful for today?

If you struggle to journal or meditate, these questions are an ideal way to get started. You can look at these questions before a meditation to quieten your mind and journal some answers. This is certainly a good tool to prevent thoughts circling when you need to rest. (There are easy mediations to get started in the online resources at the back of the book.)

Which of my behaviours is adversely affecting my life?

Can I shift my mindset to believe in myself?

Can I believe I am limitless in potential?

Can I love my future and not be stuck in the past?

Tune into the signals, using the breath or meditation. Be aware of the signs: where do they land in your body? Note any discomfort or emotion – is it pain, fear or anxiety? Identify what you are feeling to help discharge the energy behind the it.

Am I holding on to false childhood beliefs that are no longer serving me?

Can I journal my thoughts and findings to allow myself to reframe my self-belief?

What three things am I grateful for today?

Tapping
(emotional freedom technique)

Tapping with your fingertips on specific target areas, known as the twelve meridian end points, helps to calm the body. It focuses on these 'energy hot spots' to restore balance to the body's energy.

It works on similar principles as acupuncture, and sends a calming signal to the amygdala. The amygdala is the part of our brain that is on alert to keep us safe – the part of our brain that is responsible for fight-or-flight.

By activating the calmer parasympathetic nervous system, studies have shown tapping can decrease cortisol by 43 per cent, anxiety by 58 per cent and depression by 49 per cent.[57] More information in online resources.

Massage

Beyond feeling wonderful in the moment, massage has been shown to reduce breast cancer and reduce stress hormones.[58] Lymphatic massage is another form of massage that helps keep lymph ducts flowing and supports detoxification.

If you can't make it to a massage studio regularly, you can recreate some of the benefits at home. Foam rolling releases the fascia in muscles. Fascia holds our blood, nerves and muscles in place. When it is stressed our muscles tighten up and this can reduce our range of movement. Freeing up the muscles from the fascia supports muscle health and prevents compensating elsewhere, therefore promoting release and balance.

Standing barefoot on a tennis ball and rolling it around with a little pressure to massage the foot can release your fascia. Use the tennis ball to find painful areas of tightness, then rest on that point and breathe into the release.

This can be done also around the shoulder area or on the backside for the glute. You can do this by lying down on your back, placing a tennis ball between you and the floor and moving it around the areas to find areas of tension and promote release.

Yoga for anxiety

The thought of yoga may seem unappealing to you as its often associated with slim, lycra-clad, ultra-flexible women. However, yoga is a philosophy and much more diverse and inclusive than you can imagine.

Yoga is uniting movement with breath. It is a practice to settle the mind. In some Indian schools children practice yoga when they arrive to settle them down in preparation for lessons. The idea behind yoga is for us to practice our Asanas, the poses, so that we may settle our minds in preparation for meditation.

Yoga comes in many forms from highly active and dynamic to lying down in complete stillness for an entire class.

When the body is struggling with disease we are looking for Yin-like or calming practices to reduce stress and provide safety for our body. The Yang-like, powerful classes involving lots of movement, flexibility and perhaps even heat are amazing for the body and mind when we are in physical health but in a body that maybe struggling with disease this may not offer the safety and support that a calming, restorative practice can provide and may instead drive the cortisol levels higher.

The gentle practice of Yin yoga is designed to release fascia in the muscles to improve movement. All poses but one are done lying down, so it suits anyone with or without yoga experience. The position is held fully supported for a minimum of 3 minutes up to 18 minutes, although rarely held for longer than 3 minutes in a class. This allows the body to gradually relax and muscles to release from the fascia. As a Yin practice, there is always a resting pose in between each pose, however this can also be stressful to the body so it may be more beneficial to try restorative yoga to relax the body and mind, but is not intended to release fascia. It is a set of calming poses a teacher may put together for a restful relaxation and for one to enjoy.

Yoga Nidra is a beautiful meditative practice that requires you to lie still. It is entirely without movement and the teacher will lead you on a journey while you drift into the space just before sleep.

Chitta vritti nirohda

If you imagine the busy mind is represented by the ripples on a lake, the goal is to seek stillness and tranquillity – a lake with a serene, glassy surface occurs when we calm the chatter of the mind. This is the objective of yoga and meditation. Chitta vritti nirodha translates to 'the cessation (nirodha) of the mind (chitta), thoughts, or waves (vritti)'.

Sensational sleep

Sleep is a time of healing so adopting a calming bedtime routine is essential.

The glymphatic system is our detoxification system for the brain and works at night to clear waste from our brain. This elimination of waste appears to help prevent neurological disease and Alzheimer's.

Tools for sleep hygiene:

Keep food away from sleep: Aim to finish your evening meal at least 2 hours before you go to bed to help digest your food.

Take a few minutes to journal: Letting go of the day shifts thoughts from the head to the page.

Try a warm bath: Add some Epsom salts and lavender drops to unwind and towel off with magnesium oil to relax your muscles.

Keep the bedroom cool: You will sleep best in a cooler room: 16–19°C is optimum.

Avoid screen time an hour before bed: In terms of stimulation, staring at a screen is the equivalent of looking at the sun right before you want to sleep. Blue light triggers cortisol release, interferes with melatonin release and disrupts our natural circadian rhythms. If you have to use your computer in the evenings, consider installing a blue light blocker such as Iris (iristech.co/) or invest in some blue light-blocking glasses.

Avoid drinks with caffeine: No caffeine after midday as it can take up to 9 hours to break it down.

Alcohol disrupts sleep:[59] It is often easier to get to sleep after drinking alcohol, but once it is broken down in the body, it almost balances out the initial feeling of deep sleep by giving you lighter, lower-quality sleep.

Blackout blinds: We produce melatonin needed for sleep in the dark. Keeping your room dark prevents disruption to your melatonin production.

Natural bedding: Sheets made from 100 per cent organic cotton helps you avoid the chemicals used in manufacturing (POPS, mentioned previously).

Routine: Try to go to bed and get up at the same time every day so your body gets used to a healthy sleeping routine.

Turn off wi-fi: To reduce electromagnetic field pollution, which can disrupt sleep.

Avoid strenuous exercise in the evening: Conversely, some early-morning sun outside will lift your mood and help restore your circadian rhythm.

Magnesium glycinate: A lovely, easily absorbed supplement that benefits sleep and the ability to fall back asleep. Finding a brand without additives and fillers is recommended.

Mindful living

Developing a morning practice can set up your day with positivity, self-love, lowered stress hormones and good intention. Perhaps create a small positive gesture towards yourself or others, such as a Metta meditation.[60] This is a Buddhist practice for cultivating compassion for ourselves and others using loving phrases.

May I be at ease in my body, feeling the ground beneath my seat and feet.

May I be attentive and gentle toward my own discomfort and suffering.

May I be attentive and grateful for my own joy and well-being.

May I move towards others freely and with openness.

By contrast, closing the day by listing up to three things you are grateful for in a notebook kept by your bed may slow up the automatic fight-or-flight programming you fall back into the next morning.

Mindful living allows you to rewire your thoughts and supports your ability to make sustainable change. It is the pause between the action and the reaction. It is the pause to allow a mindful response to the trigger, and the more you do it the stronger the muscle gets so you can rewire the neural pathways (connections between the brain and entire nervous system).

Taking small steps to change your thoughts and perceptions will support your changes to diet and lifestyle, which in turn will gradually help you rebuild the microbiome that controls what you eat and the way that you think.

This is due to serotonin, a neurotransmitter that is made in our gut and brain when we eat healthily. Not only does it have physical effects such as reducing constipation, but it also affects us physiologically, reducing depression and creating a feeling of calm, focus, stability and happiness.

It's a cycle: we eat well, we feel good and this in turn helps us make healthy choices.

Digestion is a well-designed process in the lobster.
It has very powerful jaws which it uses to shred food. It also has
three grinding, teeth-like surfaces inside its stomach, as well as
three guts: the fore-gut to break down food, the mid-gut to absorb
food and hind-gut to eliminate waste.

Pillar 4 – The art of healing with nutrients

We have molecules in our food that instruct our genes
to turn on or turn off.

*We are what we repeatedly do. Excellence, then,
is not an act, but a habit.*

—Will Durant

Cancer and the diet

Earlier we talked about the importance of protein in the diet. To take it further, we have proteins that, when functioning correctly, can prevent tumors. They can suppress tumour growth, stop cells from dividing, and prevent tumour cells from feeding on the blood supply they need for growth.

Cancer needs a blood supply: Stress can increase our body's levels of vascular endothelial growth factor (VEGF). This is a protein that increases blood vessels, and is linked to tumour growth. Reducing stress can help combat high levels of VEGF, but we can also make changes to our diet to help keep these levels under control.[61]

Cancer damages your DNA: Another important protein is the tumour-suppressing protein p53. It attaches itself to our DNA and signals a second protein to protect the cells from dividing and forming tumours, controlling cell growth and death. With diet, we can support this vital protein to keep it healthy as it is important to help fight off cancer.

We have also learnt that carbohydrates convert to sugars and this can provide food for cancer cells and cause insulin resistance and blood sugar spikes.

While healthy fats are required for absorption of some supplements, I don't advocate a high-fat ketogenic diet that relies on animal proteins, as this puts the body under stress and is not easy to adhere to long term. Instead, I advocate for a low carbohydrate diet with healthy levels of fat and complete protein with intermittent fasting.

Foods to support p53:

Artichoke

Celery

Chamomile

Folate diet

Green tea

Oregano

Parsley

Other ways to support p53:

Exercise

Improve sleep

Lower stress

Reduce toxins

Foods to reduce VEGF:

Artichoke

Berries

Bok choy

Cacao

Citrus fruits

Garlic

Grapes

Green tea

Kale

Nutmeg

Olive oil

Parsley

Pineapple

Pumpkin

Soy beans*

Tomato

Turmeric

* Not soy products as the nutritional benefit is lost in the processing

Diet is estimated to contribute to about ⅓ of preventable cancers – about the same amount as smoking.

—Bruce Ames

Eat less, fast more

It is early days, but recent research on mammals has shown eating food of nutritional value with fewer calories than you actually need can extend life.[62]

Eating excess calories causes weight gain and is taxing on the digestive system, resulting in lethargy and ageing. It can also increase the risk of obesity, which is linked to cancer and increases the risk of death.

Eating fewer calories with adequate nutritional value also reduces the insulin-like growth factor (IGF-1) that tells your muscles and bones to grow. Past our growing phase in life, we don't need additional IGF-1 and it should be avoided, especially when it comes to cancer as it grows tumours.[63] We have become a generation of grazers, constantly consuming and not allowing the body to rest, digest and assimilate our food between meals. Snacking causes your body to keep putting energy into digestion when it could be resting or using energy and nutrients to focus on repair.

By contrast, intermittent fasting (restricting food for a period of time) has incredible benefits. It has been shown to help kill off old mitochondria (which helps to prevent disease), as well as produce new mitochondria; reduce blood pressure and resting heart rate; give the digestive system a rest; and allow the body to work on areas that need repair.

After 13 hours of fasting we exhaust our sugar stores and start burning fat. We kick-start our system into action. We kill off old mitochondria known to cause damage and at the same time encourage cell autophagy (death) and maintain quality control of our cells. We are cleaning up the body, reducing ageing and boosting immunity.

Eating in a 10-hour window, and then fasting for 14 hours overnight seems to offer the benefits mentioned above and isn't as difficult as it sounds.

You could finish your last meal at 6 or 7 pm and have your breakfast at 8 or 9 am which many of us do naturally. Eating late at night isn't ideal, as we want to eat within an hour or two of waking up to lower the stress hormone cortisol.[64]

Science has shown that fasting for longer than 14 hours on a regular basis may *not* be good for female hormones so please be mindful. Hormonal balance is compromised if the body feels unsafe: with constant long-term fasting the stress hormones are raised, the reproductive hormones plummet, libido disappears and we stop cycling – no more periods!

As a general rule, it's more beneficial to eat well 3 times a day, with a 4- to 5-hour break between each meal, and no snacking. Men generally find fasting for longer than 14 hours (16 is ideal) to be more beneficial.

Undergoing a fast for 14 to 16 hours can undo the damage that a bad diet causes. 16-hour fasts have shown to be supportive in reducing colon cancer, while breast cancer benefits from a minimum 14-hour fast.

> **For those battling cancer, fasting or eating no more than 500 calories a day consisting of vegetable juices and soups for easy digestion, one day prior to chemotherapy, on the day of treatment and the day following treatment has been shown to reduce side effects from chemotherapy and in some cases remove them all together.[65]**

The research into the 'fasting mimicking' diet has shown that reducing caloric intake while eating nutritiously before and after chemotherapy can starve cancer cells.[66]

> **Fasting is not for patients who are cachexic (have muscle wasting syndrome) and is only beneficial for those who consume a nutritional and balanced diet.**

In Dr Alejandro Junger's book, *Clean: A Revolutionary Program to Restore the Body's Natural Ability to Heal Itself,* the research shows how adopting a diet that consists of clean foods in liquid form such as smoothies and soups at either end of the day can assist with weight loss and overall heath.

Food and drink don't mix

As I mentioned earlier, digesting your food requires strong stomach acid and an acidic environment.

We want to avoid diluting digestive juices needed to break down food meaning we should avoid water 15 minutes before a meal and until 45 minutes to 1 hour following a meal. Try to drink most of your minimum 2 litres of fresh filtered water a day in hourly intervals spread out either side of breakfast and lunch.

Herbal tea is generally caffeine-free, but always check the ingredients on the box. Herbal teas are included in the recommended daily 2-litre intake of water.

Your water intake may look like this:

- Up to 500 millilitres warm water with the juice of half a lemon upon rising.
- Between breakfast and lunch, a 250-millilitre glass of water or herbal tea each hour, giving your body a rest in between.

Remember to spread out your intake to protect kidney health. It should be 3 glasses in total, and the final glass no more than 15 minutes before lunch.

– Another 2 250-millilitre glasses in the afternoon, an hour apart, and one after your evening meal and you have reached your 2-litre quota.

Quick Tip

Green tea, chai teas, matcha, coffee and caffeinated or sweetened herbal teas are not part of your 2 litres a day.

Green tea has great benefits and drinking 2–3 cups a day offers a multitude of benefits including anti-inflammatory properties which encourage the autophagy of cancer cells (cell death) and suppress the metastasis of tumours.[67]

Morning

Breakfast can and should be a nurturing, calming and positive start to the day. It reduces the stress hormone cortisol, which spikes in order to wake you up (otherwise you would remain asleep), and fuels you for the day ahead. Breakfast is the meal that provides nourishment following your overnight fast and is the most important meal of the day.

Using fresh, organic, whole food, and freshly prepared seasonal ingredients that are full of vitality, can help to harmonise the body and mind – applying a mindful approach to a crucial meal.

Mixing up breakfast options by playing with ingredients is a perfect way to get different benefits from the phytonutrients available from different foods to power you up for the day.

Taking an extra minute to two to breathe deeply and mindfully consider the food you are about to consume can transform a pit stop into a meal that nourishes body and mind.

Juices and smoothies

Juicing is the quickest way of getting a high dose of micronutrients into your body, whether you want to boost your health, are fighting disease, feeling rundown or are giving back to your body after a late night.

Juicing before a meal is a great way to fulfil your nutritional requirements. The more juicing you do, the quicker you boost your health. Some cancer clinics require patients to have 13 x 250 millilitre juices a day. Juicing vegetables is an effortless way to improve your nutrient status without the work of digestion. It can, however, be challenging in colder climates and over a long period of time, and generally cleaning juicers is what puts most of us off. The benefits are nevertheless outstanding for our health.

At the well-known Gerson Clinic for Cancer, patients on the full therapy program drink 13 x 250 millilitre fresh juices daily. It can be useful to use an organic farm delivery system for items that are not readily available in the supermarkets.

The 13 juices are made up of:
1 pure orange juice
4 green juices
5 carrot/apple juice
3 pure carrot juices

Always aim for organic for the juices where possible, otherwise refer to the Dirty Dozen/Clean 15 (page 106). These juices use a lot of vegetables and we want to avoid pesticide exposure as much as possible.

Try a different juice before each meal and drink immediately after preparation. Storing in a fridge lowers the enzyme activity of the ingredients and therefore the nutritional value, so juices are best consumed fresh.

Green
Makes 1 glass

150 g mixed watercress, red lettuce, romaine and endive
¼ green pepper
1 leaf red cabbage
2 Granny Smith apples, cores removed and quartered
1 large chard leaf

Rotate leaves and a piece of apple as you put ingredients into a juicer. Juice and drink immediately.

Orange
Makes 1 glass

5–6 large carrots
2 Granny Smith apples

Juice and drink immediately.

Omit the apple and add more carrots (6–8 large) for the 3 pure carrot juices.

Smoothies differ to juices. The fibre is removed when we juice but remains in a smoothie, so smoothies are a great way of getting fibre into the diet. Try vegetables or chia seeds – both are beneficial!

Make your own smoothie

Base liquid: Water, nut milk or coconut water for hydration. All unsweetened with no additives.

Base: Flaxseeds (omega 3), chia (fibre), hemp and pea protein (protein).

Fruit: Handful of blueberries for phytonutrients.

Vegetable: Optional half an avocado or a handful of green leaves to start your vegetable intake early in the day; avocado offers good fats and green leaves like watercress help the liver detoxify.

Blood sugar balancer: ½ tsp of Ceylon cinnamon.

Fats: Flax oil is a great source of omega 3. Nut butter and avocado are a source of fat and protein.

- Almond butter is higher in protein than hazelnut butter, for example, but it is great to swap between the two as they provide different nutrients.

- Cashews and peanuts have a higher carbohydrate content (that will convert to glucose) so it is better to avoid them and use seed butters or almond butter where possible.

- Use raw nut butters or raw nuts themselves, rather than roasted, for added nutritional benefits.

Superfoods to add to smoothies:
Bee pollen: Antibacterial and antiviral
Maca: Antioxidant
Chlorophyll: Boosts red blood cells
Spirulina: Reduces inflammation

Super Protein Smoothie
Makes 2 generous glasses

1 tbsp flax
1 tbsp chia
1 scoop clean natural hemp and pea protein powder
½ avocado
½ cup frozen berries
1 banana (optional)
1 tbsp almond nut butter or pumpkin seed butter or flax oil
1 cup clean almond milk or coconut water
1 cup filtered water
1 scoop Green powders (Synergy, Terranova life drink or Rheul)
1 handful organic watercress

Blend in a NutriBullet or blender quickly to avoid letting the ingredients reach room temperature. The frozen berries will keep it cool to lessen enzyme breakdown and ensure nutrients remain intact.

Simple Smoothie
Makes 1 glass

Thanks to Nula, Costa Rica.

1 cup coconut milk (unsweetened without additives)
1 heaped tbsp tahini
½ cup seasonal fruit, berries or papaya
1 tsp spirulina
1 handful watercress
1 tsp Ceylon cinnamon

Blend and serve immediately.

Very Berry Bowl
Makes 1 serving

Thanks to Daniella, Baja BioSana, Mexico.

2 cups frozen berries
½-cm piece of ginger, chopped
Juice of 1 orange
2 tbsp sunflower seeds, to help digestion
1 cup coconut milk

1. Cover sunflower seeds in water and soak overnight.
2. Rinse sunflower seeds.
3. Blend together ingredients, serve in a bowl and top with chia seeds, shredded coconut, goji berries and blueberries. Include cranberries for bladder support if you are prone to infections.

Activated Nuts and Seeds

Nuts, seeds and quinoa contain phytic acid which is nature's way of making them less attractive to predators and stores nutrients for their growth.

Phytic acid can cause digestive upsets, as well as preventing absorption of our minerals such as calcium, zinc, iron and magnesium, yet once broken down it can make digestion easier, allowing for greater absorption of all minerals. We don't make enough of the enzymes to break it down, but we can prepare the foods by soaking and sprouting.

It's not difficult. Simply soak nuts or seeds in filtered water with 1 tsp of freshly squeezed lemon juice overnight in a jar to reduce the phytic acid and encourage sprouting.

If you have time and want to reduce the phytic acid further, the next step is to spread them out on a tray and cook at very low temperatures (50°C) for a long period of time (8–12 hours).

This is known as dehydration and encourages sprouting as it breaks the phytic acid down even further to make them more easily digestible. A dehydrator is another option.

Soaking and sprouting times:

Almonds: 8–12 hours, 12 hours sprouting
Cashews: 6–10 hours, does not sprout
Chickpeas (Garbanzo): 12 hours, 12 hours sprouting
Mung beans: 12 hours, 2–5 days sprouting
Pecans: 6–10 hours, does not sprout
Pumpkin seeds (Pepitas): 8 hours, 1–2 days sprouting
Quinoa: 2 hours, 1–2 days sprouting
Sunflower seeds: 2 hours, 2–3 days sprouting
Walnuts: 8–12 hours, does not sprout

Daniella's Mango Tropical Bowl
Makes 1 serving

Thanks to Daniella, Baja BioSana, Mexico.

1 tbsp chia
1 tbsp flaxseed
1 tbsp quinoa, rinsed
2 cups coconut milk or water
1 cup mango, frozen
¼ tsp chopped ginger
½ tsp turmeric
Juice from ½ lemon
2 tsp sunflower seeds
1 tsp bee pollen

1. Soak the chia, flax and quinoa overnight in coconut milk or coconut water.
2. Blend together the frozen mango, ginger, turmeric and lemon.
3. Cover the soaked seeds in the mango purée and top with sunflower seeds and bee pollen.

Sunday Fry-Up
Makes 2 servings

1 bunch asparagus
1 handful cherry tomatoes, or 2 large tomatoes cut across the centre
1 large handful shiitake mushrooms
1 tbsp ghee or avocado oil
4 eggs
1 avocado
Juice from ½ lemon
Himalayan salt
1 handful rocket or baby spinach
Olive oil, to drizzle

1. Place asparagus, tomatoes and mushrooms in a roasting tin with your choice of avocado or coconut oil and cook at 180°C (fan-forced) for 20 minutes.
2. Poach eggs in water and simmer for 5 minutes.
3. Mash avocado with half a lemon and a grind of Himalayan salt.
4. Serve with a handful of rocket, drizzle with olive oil, and season with Himalayan salt and pepper for a warm weekend breakfast.

Omega 3 Cereal
Makes 2 servings

1 tbsp linseed
1 tbsp hemp seeds
1 tbsp chia seeds
½ cup berries
1 tbsp pumpkin seeds, hemp seed butter, mixed seed butter or tahini
½ tsp Ceylon cinnamon
Almond milk, to serve
Top with any quantity you like of:
Activated seeds
Shredded coconut

1. Grind the linseed and hemp seed in a coffee grinder and add to the bowl with chia seeds.
2. Top with cinnamon, warm almond milk and seeds, butters, shredded coconut, and Apple and Cinnamon Topping (see next).

Apple and Cinnamon Topping
Makes 1 serving

Use Ceylon cinnamon, otherwise labelled as Zeylanicum – it is a blood sugar balancer whereas other cinnamons are not.

1 apple
½ tsp Ceylon cinnamon
1 tsp coconut oil

1. Add coconut oil to the saucepan.
2. Roughly chop the apple and sprinkle with Ceylon cinnamon.
3. Add to a saucepan with the coconut oil and 2 tbsp water. Cover and soften for 10 minutes on low to medium heat.

Use as topping for porridge. If you also want to use frozen berries, add them into the apple mixture for a few minutes to warm.

Protein Porridge
Makes 1 serving

½ cup quinoa
1 cup hemp or almond milk
Sprinkle of Ceylon cinnamon
½ cup frozen berries

1. Rinse the quinoa and leave to soak overnight, then drain and rinse again.
2. Cook the seed, milk and frozen berries for 15 minutes on low heat; be careful not to boil.
3. Add cinnamon.
4. Serve with walnuts, and any of the toppings to follow.

Cereal and Porridge Toppings:

Seed butter of choice
Activated nuts or seeds
Shredded coconut
Cacao nibs
Apple and Cinnamon Topping (see page 190)
Tahini
Blueberries, strawberries, raspberries, blackberries

Quick Tip

Use fresh, ripe organic fruits, or frozen organic/non-organic blueberries as they are usually snap frozen when ripe so have a higher nutritional value.

Beetroot Quinoa Porridge
Makes 1 serving

Beetroot is a great liver detoxifier.

400 ml beetroot juice (ensure the beetroot is washed and peeled thoroughly before juicing to avoid any soil flavour)
½ cup quinoa
½ tsp Ceylon cinnamon
½ tsp nutmeg

1. Cook the beetroot juice and quinoa on low heat until the quinoa is soft, about 15–20 minutes.
2. Add the spices and stir in.
3. Serve with Apple and Cinnamon Topping or any of the Cereal and Porridge Toppings listed provided.

Protein Pancakes (for special occasions)
Makes 8

3 ripe bananas
3 eggs
½ cup almond butter
1 tsp Ceylon cinnamon
½ tsp vanilla
Coconut oil or avocado oil, for cooking
Mixed berries, banana or Cashew Cream, to serve

1. Mix all the batter ingredients in a blender.
2. Heat coconut oil on medium heat.
3. Add 2–3 tbsp batter for each pancake and cook on both sides.
4. Serve with berries, banana or Cashew Cream.

Cashew Cream
Makes 1 cup

This is a great alternative to dairy cream and delicious on pancakes or with chocolate mousse.

1 cup raw unsalted cashews
1 tsp vanilla extract
¼ tsp Ceylon cinnamon
Pinch of Himalayan salt

1. Soak cashews overnight and rinse.
2. Place all ingredients in a blender with ½ cup of filtered water and mix until smooth.
3. Store in a glass jar for up to 5 days.

Quick Tip
For cashew cheese, add 1 tbsp nutritional yeast, ½ tsp onion powder, ½ tsp garlic powder and remove the cinnamon and vanilla.

Chia Pudding
Makes 1 serving

1 cup almond milk
1 cup berries
1 tsp vanilla
3 tbsp chia seeds
1 tbsp cacao (optional)

Blend or mix well, then let stand for 30 minutes or overnight.

Turn this simple fibre-filled pudding or breakfast pot into a superfood by adding any of the following;

1 scoop natural unflavoured pea and hemp protein powder
1 tbsp flax oil, for omega 3
1 tsp bee pollen, to prevent metabolic disorders (chemical imbalances) such as diabetes
1 tsp maca, for energy
1 tsp Ceylon cinnamon, for blood sugar balance

Midday: Buddha Bowls

An easy way to create a healthy lunch is making a buddha bowl that contains a variety of foods, some of which can be prepared and offer a balance of fat, protein and greens. Traditionally they were vegetarian but adding a protein, animal or plant, works.

Digesting raw food takes a long time and a great deal of energy, therefore we want to eat it at lunchtime rather than in the evening to give our body time to break it down so it can absorb nutrients and eliminate fibre. Plant cells have walls, so contain lots of fibre which is good for us, so when you eat them raw, it is essential to chew each mouthful 20–40 times to break down the indigestible cellulose. If you find your digestion is slow and you feel bloated after eating, before your meal have a small digestive salad. This will help release the enzymes needed for digestion.

What's in a Buddha bowl?

Cooked mushrooms: Especially button or shiitake as they are the most medicinal of the mushrooms readily available

Homemade hummus or guacamole: Make guacamole with an avocado, half a squeezed lemon, 12 cloves of crushed garlic and Himalayan salt to taste

Broccoli sprouts: Especially for the liver; 100 grams a day if possible

Sprouted beans (organic)

Onion and garlic

Leafy greens: Especially rocket and watercress

Fermented foods: Raw sauerkraut or kimchi for gut healing

Cauliflower or quinoa tabbouleh: This is tabbouleh, substituting the gluten grain couscous for cauliflower or quinoa

Quinoa

Steamed broccoli, cauliflower or cabbage: For liver support

Asparagus: For prebiotics

Beetroot or Radish: Grated or julienned, for liver support

Herbs: To include thyme, mint, parsley, rocket and coriander

Activated nuts or seeds

Protein:

Anchovies	Mackerel
Eggs	Salmon
Goat's cheese	Sardines
Herring	Sheep's cheese

Dressings:

Coconut aminos

Flax oil, squeeze of lemon and crushed garlic

Tamari

Tahini with organic olive oil

Try and add some super seeds:

Flaxseed (crushed linseed) for omega 3

Hemp seeds for protein

Pumpkin seeds for zinc

Sunflower seeds for copper, manganese and selenium

Sesame seeds for calcium, zinc, magnesium

Quick Tip

If you don't like the monotony of a bowl of salad for lunch every day, you can put these delicious salads into a nori wrap (a sheet used for making sushi). My favourite is avocado, cauliflower tabbouleh (this version is gluten free and uses pulsed or grated cauliflower), rocket and hummus wrapped as a nori roll. Please grow or purchase organic herbs to reduce toxin exposure, creating less of a burden on your liver.

Digestive Salad
Makes 1 serving

1 tbsp organic extra virgin olive oil
1 tsp organic apple cider vinegar
½ tsp turmeric powder
Grind of black pepper
Pinch of celery salt
Handful of watercress or rocket

Whisk together the ingredients and drizzle over a bowl of rocket or watercress. Eat prior to a meal to stimulate digestion.

Avocado Bread
Makes 4 slices for 2 sandwiches

1 ripe avocado
1 egg
1 tbsp nutritional yeast

1. Preheat the oven to 180°C.
2. Mix ingredients so the avocado is not lumpy.
3. Line a baking tray with paper and spoon the mixture into 4 on the tray, flattening so each one is about 8 cm wide.
4. Cook for 20 minutes then remove and peel off from the paper.
5. The pieces are now ready to make 2 sandwiches.
6. Add your favourite ingredients. I like to spread each piece with hummus or pesto, then add rocket, tomato and basil, and season.
7. Chop in half and enjoy .

Tahini Bread
Makes 1 loaf

This is an easy, delicious bread recipe that is high in protein and good fats.

3 eggs
1 cup (250 g) tahini (use a jar and stir in the liquid on top so the tahini is runny)
⅓ cup nut milk (without oils or additives)
¼ cup coconut flour
1 cup almond flour
1 tsp Himalayan salt
3 level tsp baking powder

1. Line a loaf-shaped cake tin with baking paper.
2. Preheat the oven to 180°C.
3. Use a beater to beat eggs until frothy.
4. Add nut milk and tahini and mix with the eggs to make a batter.
5. In a separate bowl, mix the dry ingredients.
6. Stir dry ingredients into the batter, and mix until sticky.
7. Spoon the mixture into the cake tin.
8. Flatten mixture with a spatula and cover in seeds of your choice.
9. Bake in the middle of the oven for 40 minutes.

Super Seed Omega Crackers
Makes two 20 cm x 30 cm trays

6 tbsp pumpkin seeds (or 3 tbsp pumpkin seeds and 3 tbsp sunflower seeds)
1 cup flaxseeds
3 tbsp chia
2 tbsp dried thyme, rosemary or other herb
Himalayan salt

1. Mix together the seeds with 1 cup water and allow to soak for 15 minutes.
2. Mix in the thyme or other herbs to the bowl of seeds – or feel free to split the mixture and do one batch of thyme and one of rosemary or any other herb of choice.
3. Line an oven tray with baking paper and spread mixture out. Grind a little Himalayan salt or celery salt over the mixture.
4. Mark into squares and cook at 160°C (fan-forced) for 15 minutes. Turn over and bake for a further 15 minutes.
5. Cool and break into pieces. Store in an air-tight container.

Rosemary and Thyme Protein Crackers
Makes 16

100 g hemp seeds
100 g crushed linseed (flaxseeds) – give them a quick whiz in a coffee grinder or NutriBullet so they are easy to digest
2 tsp dried thyme
2 tsp rosemary
Himalayan salt

1. Mix the hemp seeds and linseed with 200 ml water and let it soak for 5–10 minutes until it becomes thick and gel-like, as this will keep the mixture from sticking to the sheet.
2. Place the mixture on a lined baking tray. Sprinkle with herbs.
3. Cover in baking paper or a silicon sheet and roll out flat.
4. Remove the top sheet and sprinkle the mixture with salt.
5. Bake in the oven for 18 minutes at 160°C (fan-forced).
6. Once cool, break into pieces and enjoy with hummus or guacamole, or store in an air-tight container.

Quick Tip
Cooking at 90°C (fan-forced) for 45 minutes to 1 hour on either side will ensure a higher nutrient status.

Hummus
Makes 1 small bowl

Some people find chickpeas (garbanzo beans) difficult to digest so we can replace them with cannellini or butter beans. Hummus is great served with slices of cucumber, radish, carrots or peppers.

75 g organic cannellini beans
1 tbsp tahini
¼ cup olive oil
Pinch of cumin
¼ cup flax oil

1. Prepare the beans. Tinned beans will be cooked and need nothing more than a rinse. Organic dried beans require 5 hours soaking and rising prior to cooking for an hour or more until soft. Strain and keep the water.
2. Mix all the ingredients and a little of the water in a food processor (I use a Vitamix or NutriBullet for smaller quantities), adding a little water gradually for a creamy consistency.
3. You can punch up the flavour by squeezing ½ a lemon into the mix or adding coriander to your liking.

Courgette Hummus (bean free)
Makes 2 servings

100 g sesame seeds
300 g courgettes, grated or finely chopped
Juice from 1 lemon (about 20 ml)
20 g tahini
1 clove garlic
50 ml olive oil
½ tsp cumin
½ tsp paprika
½ tsp Himalayan salt
¼ tsp cayenne

Place all the ingredients in a mixer and blend until a smooth mixture is formed.

Beetroot Hummus
Makes 1 small bowl for crudités

1 large beetroot
2 cups cooked cannellini beans
1 tsp coconut oil
⅓ cup lemon juice
¼ cup tahini
1–2 cloves garlic, crushed
¼ cup olive oil
Grind of Himalayan salt

1. Wash the beetroot thoroughly, chop into chunks and place in the oven with coconut oil. Cook at 180°C until it can be pierced with a fork.
2. Pulse the rest of the ingredients in a blender or food processor and loosen with additional olive oil if required. Add the beetroot and blend to your desired texture. Season to taste.

Walnut Pâté

Makes 2 servings

150 g activated walnuts
30 ml tamari
½ small onion, chopped
1 stick celery, chopped

1. Soak the walnuts overnight, then rinse and cook them at 50°C (fan-assisted) for 10 hours.
2. Place all the ingredients in a blender until you achieve the desired consistency, leaving some texture.
3. Serve with Super Seed Omega Crackers (see page 203).

Kale Crisps
Makes 1 big bowl

1 bag organic kale
Organic extra virgin olive oil
Himalayan or celery salt
Cashew cheese

1. Wash kale and remove woody stalks.
2. Tear up leaves to 5cm pieces and place in a bowl. Cover in olive oil and salt, or cashew cheese.
3. Rub into the leaves to coat them and spread out on trays in the oven.
4. Bake at 50°C (fan-assisted) for about 3 hours, until crisp.

Cauliflower Tabbouleh
Makes 6–8 servings

1 head of cauliflower, core removed and grated
1 cup chopped mint
1 cup chopped flat parsley
1 cup chopped cucumber
Seeds from 1 pomegranate
½ cup olive oil
Juice of 1 lemon
Himalayan salt and ground black pepper

Combine ingredients and enjoy!

Quick Tip
Substitute cauliflower for 2 cups of cooked quinoa.

Tricolour Spaghetti
Makes 2 servings

I make it just using courgette (zucchini) which is delicious with any of the dressings and marinades prior to serving with walnuts and basil.

1 small courgette
1 small carrot
1 small beetroot or red cabbage
Juice of 1 lemon
2 tbsp olive oil

Dressings:
Stephano's Simple Tahini Dressing or Power Pesto dressing (see page 213)
Bunch of basil and ¼ cup broken activated walnuts

1. Use a spiraliser or peeler to create long thin strands of each vegetable.
2. Toss in olive oil and lemon and let sit for 10 minutes to marinate.
3. Pile on a plate and top with pesto, tahini dressing, or fresh basil and walnuts.

Quick Tip

A spiraliser makes this dish easy; otherwise, a simple apple peeler can be used for a fettuccine-style noodle.

Kohlrabi or Courgette Salad
Makes 2 servings

In summer, when they are in abundance, I love to thinly slice courgettes and leave them to marinate in walnut oil, lemon juice, crushed garlic and a sprinkle of chilli flakes, salt and pepper. I serve them with pickled walnuts and basil to create a delicious starter. If you want to boost your liver health, then use thinly sliced kohlrabi instead.

1 kohlrabi or 2 courgettes
Juice of 1 lemon
2 tbsp hazelnut or walnut oil
1 clove garlic
1 tbsp pickled walnuts
1 tbsp chopped olives
1 tsp dried thyme
A pinch of chilli flakes
Serve on a base of rocket

1. Peel the kohlrabi.
2. Cut the kohlrabi with a vegetable peeler into very thin slices.
3. Lay the slices out on a big plate.
4. Make a dressing of the walnut oil (or hazelnut oil), lemon juice, crushed garlic, chilli flakes, thyme and season with salt and pepper.
5. Sprinkle over the chopped olives, drizzle on a little dressing and let it marinate for 10 minutes, Place a handful of rocket on top and a splash of dressing and enjoy.

Stephano's Simple Tahini Dressing
Makes 2 servings

Thanks to Stephano, Baja BioSana, Mexico.

1 heaped tbsp tahini
Grind of Himalayan salt
Big pinch of garlic powder or 1 garlic clove, crushed

Whisk ingredients together, adding water to loosen to your desired consistency.

Quick Tip
Add dill, parsley and lemon for a tasty twist to this dressing.

Curried Tahini Sauce
Makes 2 servings

1 heaped tbsp tahini
1 clove garlic
½ tsp mild curry powder
½ tsp cumin powder
2 tbsp olive oil

Mix together with enough olive oil and water to loosen. Spoon over steamed vegetables.

Power Pesto
Makes 2 servings

This delicious sauce functions as herbal medicine.

30 g bunch of mixed leaves: basil, nettle, dandelion and rocket
2 tbsp pumpkin seeds
¼ cup olive oil or flax oil
1 clove garlic
Pinch of Himalayan salt

Blend together and serve over steamed vegetables, spiralised courgette or Tricolour Spaghetti (see page 211).

Quick Tip
- Dandelion is great for potassium, is kidney cleansing and as a bitter plant also supports digestion.
- Nettle contains iron.
- Rocket boosts liver health.
- Pumpkin seeds contain zinc.
- Flax oil contains omega 3.

Sundried Pesto

Use the same recipe for Power Pesto but add 1 cup of sundried tomatoes (without additives or sugar) and halve the quantity of basil or other leaves. It is quick and easy and can be stored in a jar in the fridge for up to 10 days.

Tacos
Makes 3–4

1 ½ cups sunflower seeds, or 1 cup sunflower seeds and ½ cup walnuts activated if possible

¼ cup sundried tomatoes

2 cloves garlic, crushed

1 tsp dried oregano

¼ tsp paprika

1 tsp cumin

Pinch of Himalayan salt

2 tsp tamari

Juice of ½ lemon

To serve:
1 romaine lettuce
Small handful of coriander, bottom of stalks removed
1 avocado

1. Blend the seeds, sundried tomatoes, garlic, spices, tamari and lemon juice roughly, so the mixture still has a chunky texture.
2. Serve on a romaine lettuce leaf 'taco' with chopped avocado and coriander leaves to top.

Colourful Coleslaw
Makes 1 serving

1 raw beetroot, washed, scrubbed and peeled
½ cup cabbage, chopped
½ carrot

For the dressing:
2 tbsp flax oil or olive oil
Juice of 1 lemon
1 clove garlic, crushed
Pepper and celery salt

Toppings:
Coriander seeds and leaves

1. Finely julienne the vegetables with a mandolin or in a food processor and combine.
2. Whisk the ingredients for the dressing and pour over the vegetables to coat and let marinate for at least 10 minutes.
3. Top with seeds and coriander.
4. Enjoy with half an avocado or freshly prepared hummus.

Quick Medicinal Salad
Makes 4 servings

60–80 g bag organic rocket
200 g kimchi
3 avocados
1 tbsp ghee
300 g mushrooms
6 tbsp toasted seeds
Tahini dressing

1. Wash rocket, drain and spread on a platter.
2. Slice and cook mushrooms in ghee until soft allow to cool.
3. Slice avocado.
4. Toast seeds in a dry pan for 5 minutes until they smell toasted.
5. On the rocket spread the kimchi, then the mushrooms and sliced avocado, top with seeds and dress with dressing of choice.

Superfood Salad
Makes 4 servings

If you have had enough carbs that day then the butternut squash can be removed as it provides 20 grams of carbohydrate per person in this dish and the same applies for the feta if you have had enough animal protein.

400 g butternut squash
6 tbsp olive oil
Pinch each of cinnamon, coriander flakes and chilli flakes
300 g broccoli
200 g quinoa
1 bunch fresh coriander, roughly chopped
1 punnet rocket or salad cress (if using watercress then remove stalks)
1 ripe avocado, chopped into bite-sized pieces
200 g broccoli sprouts
3 tbsp unsalted seed mix or flaked almonds
1 pomegranate
2 tsp apple cider or balsamic vinegar
Juice of 2 limes or lemons
20 g feta

1. Wash the butternut squash and chop into small chunks.

2. Toss these in a bowl and coat with the olive oil, the cinnamon, dried coriander and dried chilli flakes.

3. Arrange the squash on a lined baking sheet and cook at 180°C (fan-assisted) for 25 minutes, then leave to cool.

4. Break the broccoli into small florets and steam for 3 minutes, then cool.

5. Rinse the quinoa and add to a pan with 600 g water, bring to the boil and then reduce to medium heat for 10 minutes. Drop to low heat until the water has evaporated and the quinoa is fluffy, and allow it to cool.

6. Place the quinoa, potato, fresh coriander, rocket or watercress, chopped avocado and sprouts into a large serving bowl.

7. Toast the seeds or almonds in a dry frying pan on a medium heat for 5 minutes, stirring constantly to prevent burning. When you can smell them toasting, remove from heat and cool before adding to the serving bowl.

8. Squeeze the pomegranate, adding the juice and seeds into the serving bowl, removing any of the white pith that drops in.

9. Mix the remaining 3 tbsp olive oil with the vinegar and lime or lemon juice, then drizzle over the salad.

10. Crumble the feta over the top and serve.

Evening

|

Evening meals should be light and easy to digest. A soup or a bowl of steamed vegetables is a great option. Some people even thrive on a protein smoothie as an evening option to ease digestion and prepare for the overnight fast.

If you are dining out and unsure what to order, most restaurants are happy to serve a piece of grilled fish or meat with steamed vegetables, with a dressing of olive oil and lemon. Many offer a selection of side vegetables.

Restaurants tend to be receptive to people with allergies and happy to oblige nowadays. Remind them when you order that you don't want sweeteners such as honey or sugar in sauces. Sushi rice typically contains sugar so is best avoided. Vegetable soups are an option if they do not contain flours, dairy or sweeteners.

Quick Tip

Carrying a few snacks is always a good idea. Some activated nuts or seeds, even a small jar of tamari to add to steamed vegetables or fish, make a delicious addition to any plain meal.

Once you are no longer fuelling the sugar-loving bacteria, you will prefer the fresh flavours of good olive oil and lemon and seasoning to other, less healthy alternatives.

Soup Base/Vegetable Stock

Makes 2 servings; 1 L

1 carrot
1 stick celery
1 onion
1 tbsp coconut oil or ghee
Few sprigs of thyme
Pinch of Himalayan salt
Pinch of pepper
1 clove garlic (optional)

1. Wash, peel and dice the vegetables.
2. Add the vegetables to a pan with coconut oil or ghee, thyme and seasoning.
3. Cook on medium heat for 5 minutes.
4. Add 1 litre of filtered water and simmer for 20 minutes.
5. When making soup just add vegetables of your choice to this base and cook over medium heat, not to the boil. Blend if a smooth consistency is desired.

Stock can be stored in the refrigerator for 3 days or frozen.

Hippocrates Soup
Makes 4 servings

At the Gerson Clinic, Mexico, where this recipe originated, this soup is taken twice a day with up to 12 juices.

1 leek
1 celeriac
500 g potato
500 g onion
500 g tomatoes
30 g parsley

Cut all the vegetables into cubes, cover with filtered water and slow cook on low heat for 2 hours.

Fennel and Lemon Alkaline Soup
Makes 2 servings

1 L Soup Base (see page 224)
1 large fennel bulb (or 2 small)
2 lemons
1 big pinch dried oregano
1 clove garlic, crushed (optional)
Handful of rocket (optional)
½ avocado (optional)

1. Grate 1 or 2 fennel bulbs into the soup base and add the juice of 2 lemons, oregano and garlic.
2. Warm gently for 10 minutes.
3. This soup is best blended with a hand blender as the fennel is coarse.

Optional
Off the heat, stir in garlic, rocket and diced avocado for added nutrition.

Tuscan Soup
Makes 2 servings

This delicious, hearty soup can be adjusted to include whatever organic vegetables are in season.

1 litre Soup Base (see page 224)
1 clove garlic (optional)
Seasonal vegetables chopped to bite size (try courgette, asparagus, mushroom, broccoli, cauliflower and/or beans)
Seasonal greens (rocket, mustard greens or cabbage)
½ avocado
Sprinkle of seeds
Olive oil, to drizzle

1. Add the vegetables to the Soup Base (not the seasonal greens), starting with those that will take the longest to cook.
2. Add a litre of water or more to cover the vegetables.
3. Cook on medium heat without boiling for 10 minutes.
4. Remove from heat and add your finely chopped leafy greens and stir to gently warm.
5. To bulk this up further, add in a little cubed avocado for good fat.
6. Cover with seeds and a splash of olive oil. Season and serve.

Just a little legumes

Lentils and Beans, known as legumes, are a delicious and nutritious way to add protein to soups and stews. However, legumes contain glutamine. Just as the growth hormones in animal proteins can contribute to cancer, glutamine also causes growth. Just like we try to keep animal products to 5 per cent or less of our diet, keeping our diet low in legumes is a good idea.

Legumes are a source of lectins that can reduce the absorption of protein and minerals. If you are using dried beans, first soak them overnight, then rinse and cook or, if you have time, leave out to dry somewhere warm to sprout for easier digestion.

Legumes are rich in polyphenols (micronutrients), and the high flavonoid and fibre content of lentils also plays a significant role in gut mobility (how well food moves through the gut). Studies have shown lentils help to reduce blood glucose levels and disease, specifically diabetes. They help build the microbiome, and unlike beans, dried lentils do not have to be soaked.

It is essential to rinse them before you cook, and if you do have time to soak them in advance, this will speed up cooking time. 100 grams of lentils provides approximately 9 grams of protein and 10–18 grams of fibre, as well as minerals such as calcium and potassium.[68] These legume recipes are great for winter but best for those who have a clear cancer diagnosis, otherwise served on an occasional basis as a warming nurturing stew.

Protein content per 100 grams for lentils, black, navy and pinto beans is approximately 8–9 grams. These beans have the lowest glutamate so are the preferred choice.

With a little forethought it is easy to prepare dried beans at home, ready to include in your next dish.

If you have time and space prior to cooking, soak the beans overnight, and find somewhere warm where you can spread them out for 24 hours to start to sprout, making them more digestible. Spread them out on a tea towel and cover with another tea towel.

Different beans have different cooking times, so check regularly until they are soft (but not mushy) and cooked through. Drain and enjoy!

Quick Tip
– Organic sauces without sugar or additives can be added to lentils to make a Bolognese, or add olives and capers for a quick parmigiana sauce. Enjoy over lightly steamed vegetables.
– Turning your Tuscan Soup into a stew is simple.
  – Add 1 cup cooked beans or lentils to the Tuscan Soup (page 227).
  – Drizzle with olive oil, and top with a handful of coriander.

Paloma's Red Lentil Chilli with Black and White Quinoa
Makes 4 servings

1 tbsp ghee
1 medium onion
1 bell pepper
1 courgette
2 garlic cloves
1 tbsp smoked paprika
1 tsp chilli flakes
1 tsp fresh grated turmeric
1 tsp thyme
1 tbsp tomato paste
400 g chopped tomatoes
400 g black beans
500 ml vegetable stock
200 g red split lentils
1 cup white quinoa
1 cup black quinoa
Himalayan Salt
Pepper

1. Heat the ghee in a large saucepan over a medium heat and fry the onions until translucent (3 minutes). Stir frequently.
2. Add the courgette and pepper and fry until softened (5 minutes) on medium heat.

3. Add the garlic and spices (paprika, turmeric, chilli flakes, thyme) and stir.

4. Add the chopped tomatoes, stock and tomato paste.

5. Stir in the lentils, then cover with a lid and simmer for 15 minutes.

6. Add the black beans and ½ cup filtered water, re-cover and simmer for another 10 minutes.

7. Add salt and pepper to taste.

8. Cook the quinoa for 10 minutes in twice the amount of water to absorb on medium heat.

9. Serve the chili on a bed of quinoa. Top with coriander and a drizzle of olive oil.

Portobello Mushroom and Chimichurri
Makes 3–4 servings

If you want to change it up, the mushrooms can be replaced with a whole green cabbage cut into quarters and roasted with just the paprika and ghee.

½ garlic bulb
Ghee or coconut oil
1 tbsp tamari
1 tsp smoked paprika
1 tsp cumin
300 g Portobello mushrooms
400 g butter beans or chickpeas (optional)
Juice of ½ lemon
3 tbsp warm water
1 tbsp olive oil

Chimichurri (optional)
30 g bunch flat leaf parsley
¼ tsp chilli flakes
1 shallot
1 tbsp chopped capers
1 tbsp apple cider vinegar
3 tbsp olive oil
Juice from ½ lemon

1. Preheat the oven to 180°C.
2. Mix the tamari and spices with a splash of water.
3. Pour a tbsp of mixture into each mushroom and place a knob of ghee or 1 tsp coconut oil on top.
4. Place on the baking tray along with the garlic bulb and roast for 25 minutes.
5. Try and spoon any liquid back into the mushrooms to serve.

Make the chimichurri
6. Finely chop the parsley and add to a bowl with remaining ingredients.
7. Add the beans or chickpeas to a blender with the lemon juice, warm water and olive oil.
8. Take the garlic from the oven and squeeze out into the beans.
9. Add more water to loosen if required
10. Serve the bean puree on a plate, top with mushrooms and drizzle with chimichurri. Enjoy.

Mung Dahl
Makes 4 servings (freeze in portions)

250 g mung beans
3/4 litre filtered water, vegetable stock or bone broth
½ tbsp ground turmeric
½ tbsp ground cumin
1 tbsp ground coriander
3 cardamom pods, smashed open
½ tbsp coconut oil or ghee
2 large onions, finely chopped
3 cloves garlic, finely chopped
1 cm ginger, peeled and finely chopped
2 carrots, diced
1 sticks celery
2 handfuls coriander, finely chopped (keep stems and leaves separate)
2 handfuls watercress
½ tbsp tamari
Grind of Himalayan salt and ground black pepper
Juice of a lime or lemon

1. Soak the mung beans for a minimum of 4 hours before rinsing.
2. Add mung beans to the water or stock, bring to the boil and then simmer, covered, for 20 minutes.

3. Add the spices to a dry frying pan and fry for 1 minute on medium heat.

4. Add the coconut oil to the pan, and fry the onions until soft.

5. Add garlic and ginger and cook for 5 minutes, stirring frequently.

6. Add the contents of the frying pan to the mung beans, along with the carrots, celery, coriander stems, tamari, salt and pepper.

7. Replace the lid and cook for 15 minutes on medium heat until carrots are soft. Stir to prevent sticking and add more water if necessary.

8. Stir in chopped watercress (stalks removed) just before serving, and top with coriander leaves and juice of the lemons or limes.

Cauliflower Steaks
Makes 2 or 3 servings; depending on size of cauliflower

Not only is cauliflower great for the liver, it is also full of folate (expectant mums, this is for you), and vitamins C, B1, B2, B3, B5, B6 and omega 3.

1 tbsp coconut oil or ghee
¼ tsp turmeric
¼ tsp cardamom (crushed with shells removed)
1 tbsp mild curry powder
1 cauliflower
Handful of rocket or watercress
¼ avocado
Olive oil, to drizzle

1. Add the coconut oil or ghee and spices to the pan on medium heat.
2. Slice the cauliflower into 1 ½ cm-thick steaks (any broken bits can also be used).
3. Place the steaks in the pan and move around to coat on both sides with the warmed oiled spices.
4. Cover and cook for 5 minutes, then turn over. The pan must not be too hot or the spices will burn, but hot enough to create crispy spiced edges on the steaks. When the cauliflower feels a little soft, it is ready.
5. Serve on a bed of rocket or a mix of watercress and rocket, top with cubed avocado and drizzled olive oil.

Ayurvedic Spice Mix
Makes ½ cup

6 tsp turmeric
3 tsp cumin
3 tsp coriander seed
6 tsp fennel seed
1 tsp ground ginger
1 tsp ground black pepper
¼ tsp cinnamon

1. Add the spices to a frying pan and dry fry (no oil) over medium heat for 10 minutes, stirring not to burn.
2. Grind the spices to a powder, cool and then store in a jar for up to 6 months.

Heavenly Cauliflower Rice with Ayurvedic Spices
Makes 3–4 side portions

Cauliflower rice is a fantastic way to improve health and decrease unnecessary carbs.

1 tbsp coconut oil or ghee
2 tsp Ayurvedic Spice Mix (see previous page)
1 cauliflower

1. Heat the oil and spice mix in a pan over a low to medium heat.
2. Grate the cauliflower and throw it into the pan, stirring to coat it in the warm spice mix.
3. Cook for 5 minutes and serve with salad, hemp hearts and seeds.

Cauliflower Curry
Makes 4–6 servings

The roasted cauliflower in this recipe is delicious on its own, but even more satisfying in a hearty curry.

1 large cauliflower
1 tsp garam masala (plus extra to sprinkle over the cauliflower for roasting)
3 shallots
3 cloves garlic
5 cm piece of ginger
1 turmeric root
1 tbsp coconut oil or ghee
300 g cherry tomatoes or 1 courgette
400 ml coconut milk
200 g baby spinach (remove stalks if using regular spinach)

1. Preheat the oven to 120°C (fan-assisted).
2. Chop the cauliflower into florets and sprinkle with garam masala. Roast for 20 minutes. (If you are short on time, then do not pre-cook the cauliflower. Just finely chop into small florets and throw in the pan with the tomatoes.)
3. Blend shallots, garlic, ginger, tumeric, 2 tbsp water and 1 tsp garam masala into a curry paste.

4. Heat the coconut oil or ghee in a pan over medium heat. Add 2 tbsp of the curry paste and stir, to avoid it sticking.

5. Chop the tomatoes in half and add to the pan, stirring to coat them in the curry paste.

6. Add the coconut milk and bring the mix to a near-boil, then add the roasted cauliflower and simmer for 20 minutes.

7. Throw in the washed spinach. Cover the pan for 3 minutes, until the spinach has just wilted. Serve and enjoy.

Note

Based on your dietary requirements, you can substitute the cauliflower for other vegetables, such as butternut squash, sweet potato, courgette, or a mixture of all three. These vegetables do not require pre-cooking. Adding chickpeas or white beans is an option also to add more protein.

Mushrooms

(Mycotherapy)

Mushrooms are a true superfood. Shiitake, maitake, reishi, cordyceps and turkey tail contain rich sources of ergothioneine, which protects us against cancer.

We can't make ergothioneine ourselves and our supplies decrease from around the age of 60. A meta-analysis pulling together results from seven studies at Penn University of Medicine concluded that eating 18 grams of mushrooms a day reduced the risk of cancer by 45 per cent compared to eating none at all.[69]

Button mushrooms and Portobello are good sources and are readily available. On the other hand, there are many studies that show the benefits of the four mushrooms below that can be taken in supplement form, unless you are in Japan where they are more likely to be found as part of the diet.

Reishi, often referred to as the 'mushroom of eternal youth', is said to improve sleep quality, reduce oxidative stress, and have anti-inflammatory and antidepressant effects. Additionally, it aids in liver detoxification, hormone modulation, stress management and mood enhancement, and has a calming impact on the nervous system.

Cordyceps mushrooms are renowned for boosting energy, vitality, and providing kidney and lung protection, along with aiding in the prevention of altitude sickness.

Lion's mane is known to support nerve remyelination (Myelin is the nerve coating that protects our nerves and is damaged in multiple sclerosis), reduce cognitive decline, and heal the lining of the digestive tract, as well as having anti-inflammatory and anti-tumour effects.

Turkey tail has been shown to stop the growth of pancreatic cancer cells in a study at Lund University, Sweden, as well as having strong antiviral capabilities.[70]

Brussels Sprouts and Shiitake
Makes 3–4 servings

200 g Brussels sprouts (or cabbage)
1 tbsp coconut oil or ghee
200 g shiitake mushrooms
1–2 cloves garlic (optional)
Himalayan salt and ground black pepper

1. Use a mandolin to slice the Brussels sprouts, or finely chop by hand.
2. In a pan, heat the coconut oil or ghee, add the roughly chopped mushrooms and garlic, and season.
3. Leave to cook on medium heat for 5 minutes, then add the Brussels sprouts and toss for another 5 minutes. Serve.

Cauliflower-Based Pizza with Mushrooms and Truffle Oil
Makes 2 servings

This is a recipe I picked up in Baja, Mexico at the Modern Elder Academy. It was prepared every Thursday for us in a beautiful stone oven outside and they generously shared the recipe with me.

1 whole cauliflower
2 tbsp hemp, almond or quinoa flour
1 egg
Salt and pepper
250 g mushrooms, sliced
Truffle oil
Handful of rocket

1. Bring a pot of salted water to the boil.
2. Break the cauliflower up into florets and simmer, covered, for 15 minutes.
3. Drain and allow the cauliflower to dry as much as possible, preferably for several hours or overnight so it isn't too wet.
4. Mix the flour, egg, salt and pepper, and the florets to make a batter.
5. Spread out on to a baking tray lined with baking paper.
6. Bake in an oven preheated to 180°C (fan-assisted) for 15 minutes.

7. Turn over and add toppings such as rocket, mushrooms pre-cooked in butter or ghee, and a good splash of truffle oil, or pesto with cherry tomatoes and grated sheep or goat's cheese. I love manchego for this.

8. Put back in the oven for 10 minutes to warm.

Stephano's Melanzane alla Parmigiana
Makes 4–6 servings

Thanks to Stephano, Baja BioSana, Mexico.

2 tbsp olive oil
1 onion, finely chopped
2 cloves garlic, minced
1 kg ripened tomatoes
2 tbsp capers
30 g basil
6 aubergines
Himalayan salt
200 g pecorino
Cashew Cream (see page 195), optional

1. Heat the olive oil in a pot over a low to medium heat.
2. Add the onion and cook until it softens, about 10 minutes.
3. Add the garlic and stir for about 2 minutes.
4. Add the tomatoes, capers and basil and stir to combine. Cook over a low heat for about 1 hour until the flavours have combined, checking it remains liquid and doesn't dry out.
5. Preheat the oven to 180°C (fan-assisted).

6. Slice the aubergines lengthways, ½ cm thick, and place them on a lined baking tray. Sprinkle with Himalayan salt to remove any bitterness, and bake in the oven for 20 minutes.

7. Once they are cool enough to handle, place a layer of aubergine slices in a casserole dish, spooning over some tomato sauce to cover and follow with a generous grate of the pecorino and/or some Cashew Cream.

8. Add more layers in the same order and finish with cheese on top.

9. Cook in the oven for 15–20 minutes at 180°C (fan-assisted) until the cheese is melted.

Quick Tip

– You can also use organic, sugar-free tomato and basil sauce, if you don't have time to make your own. I recommend an authentic Italian olive and caper pasta sauce without tomato paste.

– This recipe is made with nightshade vegetables, tomatoes and aubergine (eggplant) that contain lectins so peeling and deseeding nightshades is best to reduce lectins which are also further reduced with cooking, however this is so delicious that I had to put it in.

Something sweet for a very occasional treat

Chocolate Avocado Mousse
Makes 2 servings

2 dates
1 avocado
½ banana
1 tbsp cacao powder

To serve:
Cashew Cream (see page 195)
Fresh berries

1. Add the dates and 1 cup water to a pot, and warm on the stove for 10 minutes on medium heat until the dates soften and you can remove the seeds.
2. Place the now seedless dates and water with all other ingredients into a blender or NutriBullet and blend.
3. Serve covered in Cashew Cream and fresh berries.

Sweet Potato Brownie
Makes 12

1 cup sweet potato, cooked and mashed
½ cup almond or peanut butter, unsweetened
2 tbsp lucuma
¼ cup cacao powder

1. Blend all ingredients and spread the mix on a greased baking tray.
2. Mark into squares so they are easy to break up when cooked and cook in a preheated oven at 180°C (fan-forced) for 20 minutes.

Lobsters mainly feed on fresh marine life and after feeding, to protect their resting place, they bury any left-over food in the sand, away from their base.

A holistic path

Discover what brings you fulfilment, joy, and a sense of purpose and combine it with the desire to experiment and grow along the way.

It may blossom and change as you navigate life's journey to align with your unique needs to create a wholesome and happier outlook assisting your healing and well-being.

If I could define enlightenment briefly,
I would say it is 'the quiet acceptance of what is'.

—Wayne Dyer

Recipe for life

A 'recipe for life' is a set of principles and practices to help live a fulfilling and meaningful life. It is unique to you and involves embracing a holistic approach that addresses physical, mental, emotional and spiritual well-being.

Some of the key ingredients may include:

Mindfulness and acceptance: Cultivate mindfulness and acceptance of the present moment to create a peaceful existence. The ability to be fully present and engaged in each moment without judgement, accepting the situation as it is, helps avoid suffering.

Positive relationships: Form and maintain meaningful relationships with friends, family, and a supportive community. Social connections contribute to a sense of belonging and happiness.

Continuous learning: Embrace a growth mindset and a willingness to learn and adapt. Engaging in lifelong learning keeps your mind active and engaged.

Purpose and passion: Pursue activities and goals that align with your values and passions. Having a sense of purpose adds meaning and motivation to your life. Pursue what lights you up, what makes you feel alive. It may be creative pursuits you have always put aside or volunteering for a cause you are passionate about.

Gratitude and joy: Practise gratitude daily and find joy in simple pleasures. Gratitude fosters a positive outlook and enhances overall well-being.

Stress management: Develop healthy coping mechanisms for managing stress, such as deep breathing, meditation, and relaxation techniques.

Kindness and compassion: Extend kindness and compassion to yourself and others. Acts of kindness foster positive emotions and create a sense of connection to all around you.

Emotional resilience: Build emotional resilience by developing the skills to navigate challenges and setbacks may improve meaningful relationships that offer support and promote a stronger sense of belonging.

Love: Cultivate and nurture relationships with loved ones. Express love and gratitude to those around you, and prioritise spending quality time with family and friends.

Self-care: Prioritise your physical health by eating a balanced diet, staying hydrated, exercising regularly, and getting enough sleep. Nurturing your body directly impacts your overall well-being.

Healthy diet: Fuel your body with a balanced and nutritious diet. Incorporate a variety of whole foods, including fruits, vegetables, lean proteins, nuts, seeds, and healthy fats. Prioritise hydration and avoid consumption of processed and sugary foods.

Exercise: Regular physical activity is crucial for maintaining physical and mental well-being. Find exercise routines that you enjoy, whether it's walking, occasional jogging, yoga, swimming, or dancing. Aim for consistency rather than perfection and incorporate the more yin-like or relaxed activities into your lifestyle to calm the nervous system and reduce stress hormones using conscious breathing.[71]

Radical remissions

Kelly Turner, Ph.D., is an expert in oncology and author of *Radical Remission*. She conducted a study involving people with cancer who either had not had conventional treatment (no chemotherapy, radiation or surgery) or who had tried conventional treatment but had decided to stop, either because they were told nothing more could be done, or because side effects were unbearable.

Dr Turner identified 76 different healing factors that patients used outside conventional cancer treatments. Of these, 9 stood out as common factors among all survivors.

The Nine Factors: Radical Remissions

1. Firstly there was a radical change in diet. They all adopted a predominantly plant-based diet, with a huge increase in fresh vegetables and fruit and omitting meat, wheat, sweets and dairy. Most removed alcohol and all ceased smoking.

2. They took ownership of their health, their choices of food, treatments, and behaviours.

3. They followed their intuition more closely than ever. Intuition being the inner guide or gut feeling, is 'not science- or evidence-based' and is often overlooked. They all said they had to establish the habit of trusting themselves, and take responsibility for the consequences of their intuition.

4. Almost all took nutritional supplementation that varied widely. Ranging from pro- and prebiotics to vitamins, minerals, herbs, food extracts and various food concentrates like fresh raw juices and greens. Most often they were guided by a healthcare practitioner with qualifications in nutrition who was not an oncologist, doctor or hospital dietician.

5. All worked on releasing suppressed emotions and feelings. As an extension of trusting their intuition, they learnt to believe they were free and safe to be themselves. Some resorted to hypnotherapy, counselling, psycho-therapy, group meetings, workshops, courses and diving into relevant books.

6. They all made a conscious effort to increase positive emotions. They experienced and witnessed negative emotions that came up and responded mindfully knowing they could choose how to respond. They made an active choice to increase positive emotions like love, laughter, warmth, forgiveness, joy, appreciation, gratitude and compassion when doubt crept in.

7. They couldn't emphasise enough how important social support was in recovery. Social support played a big part, from loved ones, both near and far, friends, colleagues, local community, support groups and professionals.

8. They all engaged in deepening their spiritual connections. A combination of meditation, a deeper connection to nature and appreciation of the natural world. Religion may not have necessarily played a part but all felt reconnected to nature and a connection to something more powerful than themselves.

9. They had a strong reason to live. A purpose – or ikigai. This transcended a personal desire to keep going.

Just as Dr Viktor Frankl stated in his iconic book *Man's Search for Meaning*, where he shares his experience as a prisoner in Auschwitz during World War II, he concludes those who lost their reason to live died quickly.

Dr Turner noticed his patients all had a 'I do not want to die' attitude.

Dr Turner called the recoveries 'radical remission'. Radical remission was not instant, not luck, but a process involving conscious change over time.

Routine

|

The habits of successful people:

They have a morning practice.
They workout regularly.
They meditate.
They journal, and track events.
They make purpose-driven lists in the morning.
They plan how to avoid distraction.
They plan their day as they would like it to run.
They practise gratitude before bed.

Some suggestions for a morning routine:

Often when we are unwell and in treatment we find ourselves at a loss as to what to do. We lose our regular routine, confined by new parameters. Generally if we are unwell it is a time to rest and recharge the body and the morning routine – whether we are unwell or not – is a way to start your day with purpose, meaning and a positive mindset.

- Drink a glass of filtered warm water with the juice of half a lemon.
- Exercise for 20 minutes to 1 hour or take a brisk 30 minute walk. If walking, you may choose to listen to an audiobook: something motivational and uplifting. For those with cancer you may want to try *The Journey* by Brandon Bays or *Radical Remissions* by Dr Kelly Turner.
- Drink another warm water and lemon after your walk/workout.
- Meditate for 15–20 minutes (use Soul Sync on YouTube if you are a beginner).
- Journal: Write down 3 things you are grateful for and 1 thing that would make your day great.
- Shower: Hot, then cold if possible; alternate a few times. (See 'Contrast Therapy', page 266.)
- Pre-breakfast supplements: Some supplements are best on an empty stomach. Take prebiotics just before you eat.
- Prepare juice and breakfast smoothie: Try a green juice.
- Prep or plan lunch and supper so you have it ready.
- Drink green tea/filtered water/herbal tea.
- Enjoy your day.
- Take an infrared sauna every third day if possible for detox (see page 267).

Some suggestions for lunchtime:

– Have another green juice 15 minutes before lunch.
– Lunch: A Buddha bowl with lots of raw vegetables including protein and good fats like avocados and nuts.

Some suggestions for evenings or weekends:

– Plan a hike with friends, learn tai chi or qi gong, try yin yoga, yoga Nidra or restorative yoga.
– Massage weekly or fortnightly to reduce stress.
– Try acupuncture for pain.

Some suggestions to help you relax and reduce stress before bed:

– Make yourself a fresh juice before your evening meal.
– Try steamed vegetables or soups with plant protein for the evening meal.
– Pick up a notebook before bed and note 3 things you are grateful for and something great that happened that day.
– Aim to sleep for 7 hours minimum.

Ikigai

The Japanese secret to a long and happy life:
- Stay active, don't retire early.
- Take it slow, remove urgency.
- Don't fill your stomach; eating to 80 per cent capacity helps us live longer.
- Surround yourself with good friends who make you laugh and feed your soul.
- Get in shape for your next birthday.
- Smile – never forget the privilege it is to be here.
- Reconnect with nature.
- Give thanks.
- Live in the moment, today is what you have so make the most of it.

It may explain the extraordinary longevity of the Japanese people especially those in the Blue Zone on the island of Okinawa, specifically Ogimi. Here they enjoy Moringa tea in the morning, adopt the attitude of treating everyone as a brother, *ichariba chode* and believe in teamwork *yuimaaru*.

Follow your ikigai, your unique passion that gives meaning to your days and drives you to be the best of yourself.

Art, music and dance are elements of play. They are a beautiful escape from daily worries. There is some scientific evidence to show these activities appear to lower anxiety and increase joy.

Ayurvedic medicine

Ayurvedic medicine ('Ayurveda' for short) is one of the world's oldest holistic (whole-body) healing systems.

We can use Ayurveda to increase our energy and vitality. One of the three vital life essences is known as ojas. This is the biological energy that Ayurveda and yogic practices promote in us to give us vigour and strength. By increasing our ojas with physical vitality, we can feel youthful and vibrant.

When our ojas is low, we experience low energy, brain fog, low libido, fear, weakness, low immunity and feelings of low self-esteem.

The remaining two life essences are prana (life force and energy that governs the systems in the body: digestion, respiration, excretion) and tejas (radiance and courage; it is about the metabolism of food, healthy senses, our emotions and perceptions).

Low ojas can be attributed to:

Anxiety

Anger

Chronic pain

Constant travel

Disease

Lack of sleep

Overworking

Stress

Restoring ojas can be achieved by using yoga, particularly the breath, meditation, walking in nature, light exercise, conscious breathing and positive affirmations.

Healing modalities

We have seen there are practices we can do such as breathing, walking barefoot on the grass, meditation, walking, HIIT training or dipping in cold water. We can wake the body up so it activates cells to take action, to clean up damaged, destructive cells and boost immunity. Some of these modalities are at our disposal free of charge, others are not, but doing something is a start and opens up other possibilities.

Acupuncture:

This ancient practice helps to reduce the side effects of treatments and reduce inflammation.

During my time in Baja Mexico, I encountered an acupuncturist. Curious about his journey into this field, I inquired about his background. He shared that he had been diagnosed with colon cancer at the age of 23 and that his experience with acupuncture had remarkably alleviated his treatment-related side effects. Motivated by his personal healing, he embarked on a path of studying acupuncture and eventually took over the very practice that had played a role in his recovery. It really does work.

Contrast therapy:

Hot/cold therapy or ice baths have many positive effects on the body, activating our SIRT genes and promoting longevity. They can alter pain signals travelling to and from the brain, providing temporary relief.[72] Jump in the shower for 1 minute hot, then 10 seconds cold, or swim in a cold stream.

By directing blood towards the skin's outer layer, toxins are eliminated from the body.

Contrast therapy enhances cellular health by stimulating the production of additional mitochondria, which are the energy centres of cells. This increase in healthy mitochondria contributes to maintaining a cancer-resistant environment within the body.

Hyperthermia or thermal therapy:

This treatment heats the body tissues to 45°C to help damage or kill cancer cells. It doesn't harm healthy body tissues, and can be quite challenging. However, it is worth investigating and is used commonly in integrative cancer clinics. Integrative cancer clinics use practices such as this to support the body, alongside drugs that were initially licensed for other diseases but have shown to have anticancer action. A nutritional diet and supplements are generally part of the therapy at an integrative clinic.

Mistletoe therapy:

An injectable treatment that involves the use of extracts from the European mistletoe plant. The extracts are believed to stimulate the immune system, boosting the body's natural defences against cancer cells, and have shown to inhibit the growth of cancer cells in laboratory testing. Some patients feel an improvement in their overall well-being, experience reduced side effects from conventional cancer treatments and enhanced quality of life. Further testing is ongoing but it is worth mentioning and discussing with an oncologist.

Red light therapy (photobiomodulation):
5 to 10 minutes a day of low-level infrared light can improve muscle cell growth by 150–200 per cent, thus increasing muscle mass and improving recovery and athletic performance.[73] Red light has also been shown to increase energy production, lower inflammation and balance hormones. The bonus is it can stimulate collagen, elastin and hyaluronic acid, helping to reduce fine lines and wrinkles.[74]

Kindness

The impact of kindness and gratitude on our health is a vital component to healing. As we embark on the journey of nurturing our well-being, extending these qualities towards ourselves becomes essential.

Kindness acts as a gentle anchor, guiding us through the ebbs and flows of our health endeavours with compassion and understanding. When we treat ourselves with kindness, we create a nurturing environment that bolsters our resilience, cultivates self-acceptance, and fosters a positive outlook. Similarly, gratitude serves as a powerful catalyst, allowing us to recognise and celebrate the achievements, no matter how small, along our health journey.

Embracing gratitude empowers us to shift our focus from perceived shortcomings to the victories that propel us forward. Together, kindness and gratitude infuse our pursuit of health with an enriching sense of self-worth and optimism, creating a harmonious connection between our emotional well-being and our physical vitality. Being kind and accepting to ourselves makes us kinder and more accepting of others.

Closing words

I hope I have empowered you to take control of your health. To understand the interaction between your mindset, willpower, and gut health and how it defines your dietary choices and overall wellness.

My aim was to show you how a healthy gut microbiome will support you with the right food choices and by nurturing your 'good' bacteria through a wholesome diet, you can manage external triggers more effectively, allowing your intentions for improved health to align with your actions.

Now you are well-informed as to why you need to make conscious choices, including removing processed foods and drinks, alcohol, dairy, gluten and sugar and moderating consumption of animal products, to influence overall well-being and potentially lower the risk of disease.

By embracing alternatives that offer superior nutritional value and aligning your diet with your specific health requirements, you can achieve optimal health and vitality.

Then there are all the healing modalities, some known as biohacks, that can extend our lifespan: some of which cost us nothing!

The science behind lengthening telomeres is still evolving and much is being studied, however these lifestyle factors may contribute to maintaining telomere length or promoting their health, and may ultimately allow you to age gracefully, free of disease with confidence and courage.

Note

- It's important to emphasise that the process of telomere lengthening is complex and influenced by genetics, environment, and various factors. While adopting a healthy lifestyle is generally beneficial for overall health, no single strategy is guaranteed to significantly lengthen telomeres.

- Always consult with a healthcare provider before making significant changes to your lifestyle, especially if you have specific health concerns.

Acknowledgements

With love and deep gratitude, I want to express that this book owes its existence to an incredible circle of individuals.

To Mike, whose unwavering belief in me, this project, and our personal growth, it has been an extraordinary journey filled with love and support.

To Seb, Mark and Richard who gave valuable time to proofread and typeset.

To the remarkable and courageous women who inspire me every day:

Shannon, your invaluable support at the onset of this project brought structure and clarity to this jumble of words, making it coherent.

Tierney, who has shared this life journey with me, your inspiration, faith, and unwavering backing of this project means the world.

Annabel, my unofficial psychologist, your daily reminders of keeping my eye on the ultimate goal has kept me on track.

Tara, your strength, beauty and support has been a constant source of inspiration.

To Sarra, Libby, Kitty, Lisa, Suzann and the beautiful T16 angels – my sisters, I offer my heartfelt gratitude.

My family, my mother, and most notably my father, who discovered his passion for writing books at a late age and continues to write at 91. Your persistent enquiry of 'how is the book' has been my motivating force.

For Margaret, whose unwavering belief in me will forever be cherished, and for Todd, a resilient fighter who, like all those lost to cancer, faced an unjust fate but will always be remembered.

We miss you.

Store cupboard

Staples:

Activated nuts: almonds, cashews and walnuts

Almond butter

Aloe vera juice

Black beans

Dandelion coffee

Eggs

Essiac tea[75]

Flaxseed oil, cold pressed

Flaxseed or linseed to grind

Hemp powder

Hemp seed butter

Hummus (if you have no time to make this, buy organic)

Kimchi

Lentils

Milk, clean (no additives): almond milk or hemp milk

Mung beans

Nutritional yeast

Pumpkin seed butter

Pea protein

Quinoa

Sauerkraut

Shredded coconut

Spirulina

Sundried tomatoes

Tahini

Tomato sauces (without added sugar)

Vanilla (organic)

Fresh foods:

Apples
Asparagus
Avocado
Aubergine
Bananas
Beetroot
Berries (fresh organic or
  frozen organic): blueberries,
  strawberries, raspberries,
  blackberries, cranberries
Broccoli
Broccoli sprouts
Butternut squash
Carrots
Cherry tomatoes
Cauliflower

Coriander
Dandelion
Garlic
Ginger
Jackfruit
Kale
Lemons (1 day minimum)
Microgreens (young vegetable
  greens)
Mushrooms, organic
Mushrooms, shiitake
Red onion
Rocket
Spinach
Watercress
White onion

Organic herbs and spices:

Basil
Ceylon cinnamon
Coriander seeds
Cumin
Fennel seeds

Ground ginger
Nettle
Nutmeg
Rosemary
Turmeric root

How to grow broccoli sprouts
by Steph Gaudreau

1 L Mason jar, wide mouth, with mesh sprouting lid
2 tbsp organic broccoli sprout seeds specifically marked for sprouts
Filtered water
Glass-lock container

1. Soak the broccoli seeds.
2. Add 2 tbsp of broccoli seeds to the Mason jar.
3. Fill the jar halfway with water, and put the mesh lid on.
4. Let the jar stand at room temperature for 8 hours or overnight.
5. After 8 hours, dump out the water.
6. Place the jar into a glass-lock container (no lid) or bowl with the opening facing down and store in a dark cabinet.
7. 2 or 3 times a day, rinse and drain the sprouts. Fill the jar with fresh water, swirl it around, and drain the water out through the mesh lid. Place back in the cabinet with the opening facing down.
8. By the fourth or fifth day, your sprouts will be long enough. You'll know it's time because they've pretty much filled up the jar. Place the jar on a sunny windowsill for a couple of hours, and the sprouts will develop a nice green colour.

9. Store the broccoli sprouts: Be sure your sprouts are dry before you refrigerate them. Remove the sprouts from the jar with clean hands and spread them out for an hour or so on a kitchen towel with some paper towel on top of that, until they dry.

10. Store the sprouts in a covered glass-lock container or the Mason jar with a solid cover.

Refrigerate your sprouts for 2–3 days. After 3 days discard what's left.

Glossary

Aflatoxin: A toxic and carcinogenic substance produced by certain moulds, often found in improperly stored foods.

Anti-inflammatory: Refers to substances or actions that help reduce inflammation in the body, which is associated with many chronic diseases.

Alpha linolenic acid: An essential omega 3 fatty acid with potential health benefits for heart and brain health.

Aloe vera: A succulent plant with gel-filled leaves used for its potential soothing and healing properties.

Anaerobic respiration: Cellular respiration that occurs in the absence of oxygen, producing energy and metabolic by-products.

Arachidonic acid: A polyunsaturated fatty acid that plays a role in inflammation and is a precursor to various signalling molecules.

Assimilation: The process of absorbing and incorporating nutrients, substances, or information into the body's structure or metabolic processes.

Auto-immune disease: A condition in which the body's immune system mistakenly attacks its own cells, tissues, or organs.

Autophagy: Comes from the Greek language and means 'self-eating'. It describes the process by which cells break down and recycle their own components. Autophagy is essential for removing damaged or dysfunctional cellular structures and for maintaining overall cellular quality control.

Breathwork: Techniques involving controlled breathing patterns, often used for relaxation, stress reduction, and improved well-being.

Blood sugar: The concentration of glucose (sugar) present in the bloodstream, regulated by insulin and important for energy balance.

B vitamins: A group of essential water-soluble vitamins that play crucial roles in various bodily functions.

C reactive protein: A marker of inflammation in the body that can help assess overall health and risk of certain diseases.

Circulatory: Relating to the circulatory system, which includes the heart, blood vessels, and blood circulation.

Corn silk: The silky fibres found on corn (maize) that have been used traditionally for their potential diuretic properties.

DHA: Docosahexaenoic acid, an omega 3 fatty acid important for brain health and development.

Diuretic: A substance that increases the excretion of water and electrolytes (such as sodium and potassium) from the body through urine.

DNA: Deoxyribonucleic acid, the genetic material that contains the instructions for the development and functioning of living organisms.

Digestive: Relating to the process of breaking down food in the body and absorbing nutrients.

Earthing: Also known as grounding, it involves direct physical contact with the earth's surface, believed to have potential health benefits.

Endocrine: Referring to the glands and hormones of the body's endocrine system, which regulate various physiological processes.

Enzyme: A biological molecule that catalyses chemical reactions in the body, essential for various biochemical processes.

EPA: Eicosapentaenoic acid, an omega 3 fatty acid with potential cardiovascular benefits.

Epidemiological: The study of how diseases and health related events spread and impact populations.

Ergothioneine: An antioxidant compound found in certain foods, believed to have protective effects on cells.

Erythrocyte sedimentation rate: A marker of inflammation and certain medical conditions, determined by the rate at which red blood cells settle in a tube.

Functional medicine: An approach to healthcare that focuses on identifying and addressing the root causes of illness and promoting overall well-being.

Gastroesophageal reflux disease (GERD): A chronic digestive disorder characterised by stomach acid flowing back into the oesophagus, causing symptoms like heartburn.

Glycated haemoglobin: Also known as HbA1c, it's a measure of average blood sugar levels over a few months, used to monitor diabetes.

Holistic: Considering the whole person, including physical, mental, emotional, and spiritual aspects, when addressing health and wellness.

Hormesis: A biological phenomenon in which exposure to low or moderate levels of stress or toxins can result in a beneficial adaptive response by an organism. Rather than causing harm, these mild stressors stimulate the organism's defence mechanisms and cellular repair processes, leading to improved resilience and overall health.

Ikigai: A Japanese concept that represents the intersection of one's passion, mission, vocation, and profession, contributing to a sense of purpose and fulfilment.

Insulin-like growth factor (IGF): A hormone that plays a role in cell growth, development, and maintenance.

Insulin resistant: A condition where cells do not respond effectively to insulin, leading to high blood sugar levels and potentially type 2 diabetes.

Integumentary: Relating to the skin and its appendages (hair, nails, glands), serving various protective and regulatory functions.

Irritable bowel syndrome (IBS): A common gastrointestinal disorder characterised by abdominal pain, bloating, and changes in bowel habits.

Linoleic acid: An essential omega 6 fatty acid important for cell function and structure.

Malnutrition: A condition resulting from an inadequate or unbalanced diet, leading to health problems.

Matcha: A powdered green tea with potential health benefits due to its high concentration of antioxidants.

Metabolites: What is left when we break down nutrients for energy, building and repairing cellular structures, and eliminating waste products.

Mindset: A person's attitude, beliefs, and thought patterns, which can influence behaviour and well-being.

Mitochondria: Organelles within cells that produce energy through cellular respiration.

Microplastics: Tiny particles of plastic that have become pervasive in the environment and may have health implications.

Musculoskeletal: Relating to the muscles and bones, their structure, function, and disorders.

Naturopathic nutritionist: A professional who combines principles of naturopathy and nutrition to promote health and well-being.

Neural pathways: Specialised routes or connections formed by neurons (nerve cells) in the nervous system that allow for the transmission of electrical signals and information between different parts of the brain, spinal cord, and peripheral nervous system.

Nervous: Relating to the nervous system, which includes the brain, spinal cord, and nerves, responsible for transmitting signals and controlling bodily functions.

Neurotransmitters: Neurotransmitters are tiny messengers in the brain that help nerve cells communicate with each other. They pass signals between nerve cells to other cells, like muscles or glands. These chemicals control many things in our bodies, like mood, movement, and thinking. Examples include serotonin and dopamine.

Neuroepigenetics: The study of how epigenetic mechanisms (changes in gene expression) influence the nervous system and behaviour.

Ojas: A concept in Ayurveda representing vital energy, strength, and immunity.

Oxidation: Chemical reactions involving the loss of electrons, often associated with ageing and cellular damage.

Pharmacology: The study of drugs and their effects on the body, including interactions and mechanisms of action.

Photobiomodulation: The use of light to stimulate or modulate biological processes, potentially for therapeutic purposes.

Physiology: The study of the functions and processes of living organisms and their parts.

Prebiotics: Substances that promote the growth and activity of beneficial microorganisms in the gut.

Probiotics: Live microorganisms that may provide health benefits when consumed, often referred to as 'good' bacteria.

Remineralising: The process of restoring minerals to teeth or bones, often related to dental or bone health.

Reproductive: Relating to the organs and processes involved in reproduction and the creation of offspring.

Respiratory: Pertaining to the respiratory system, which involves breathing and the exchange of gases.

Sanskrit: An ancient Indo-Aryan language often used in traditional Indian texts and literature.

Small intestinal bacterial overgrowth (SIBO): A condition characterised by an excessive growth of bacteria in the small intestine, leading to digestive symptoms.

Sirtuins: Proteins involved in various cellular processes, including aging, metabolism, and stress resistance.

Sulforaphanes: Phytochemicals found in cruciferous vegetables that have potential health benefits, including antioxidant and anti-inflammatory properties.

Telomerase: An enzyme responsible for maintaining the length of telomeres, the protective caps at the ends of chromosomes. The regulation of telomerase activity plays a crucial role in cellular lifespan and the prevention of cellular damage.

Telomere: A region of repetitive DNA sequences located at the ends of linear chromosomes. Telomeres serve a protective function by preventing the degradation and fusion of chromosome ends, which would otherwise lead to genetic instability and cell malfunction.

With each cell division, telomeres naturally shorten, as a small portion is lost during the replication process. This gradual shortening is associated with the aging of cells and is often considered a cellular 'clock'. When telomeres become critically short, a cell may enter a state of senescence (cellular aging) or undergo programmed cell death (apoptosis). Telomeres play a vital role in maintaining genomic integrity and cellular health.

Online resources

1. Soul Sync – guided meditation on *https://www.youtube.com/watch?v=zO8tQkjCpyc&ab_channel=SriPreethaji%26SriKrishnajiYouTubeTara Brach meditations: RAIN (Recognise, Acknowledge, Inquire, Nurture), https://www.tarabrach.com/rain.*

2. Nessi Gomes – Breathwork session, 'From Darkness to Light', free on Spotify or Apple Music.

3. For breathwork on Instagram, see Stuart Sandeman, @ breathpod.

4. Emily Fletcher ZIVA Meditation, *https://zivameditation.com*

5. How to Tap with Jessica Ortner, *https://www.thetappingsolution.com/jessica-ortner/.*

6. *The Earthing Movie* is free to watch, *https://www.Groundology.co.uk.*

7. Care Oncology Clinic offers a therapeutic protocol alongside treatment.

8. Chris Wark, *www.Chrisbeatcancer.com.*

9. Joe Dispensa – YouTube has many meditations available.

Recommended reading

1. Brandon Bays (2012) *The Journey: A Practical Guide to Healing your Life and Setting Yourself Free.* Atria Books.

2. Dr Joe Dispenza (2013) *Breaking the Habit of Being Yourself: How to Lose Your Mind and Create a New One.* Hay House Inc.

3. Dr Alejandro Junger (2016) *Clean: A Revolutionary Program to Restore the Body's Natural Ability to Heal Itself.* Harper One.

4. Gabor Maté (2019) *When the Body Says No: The Hidden Cost of Stress.* Vermillion.

5. Dr Mindy Pelz (2022) *Fast Like a Girl: A Woman's Guide to Using the Healing Power of Fasting to Burn Fat, Boost Energy, and Balance Hormones.* Hay House Inc.

6. James Nestor (2020) *Breath: The New Science of a Lost Art.* Riverhead Books.

7. Peter Levine with Ann Frederick (1997) *Waking the Tiger: Healing Trauma.* North Atlantic Books.

8. Dr Kelly Turner (2014) *Radical Remission: Surviving Cancer against All Odds.* Harper One.

9. Cheryl Reid, (2005) *The Healing Power of Food: Discovering food that could save your life.* Ark House Press and Media Incorporated

References

1   Yousefzadeh, M., Henpita, C., Vyas, R., Soto-palma C., Robbins P. & Niedernhofer L. (2021). DNA damage-how and why we age? *eLife*, vol. 29(10). *https://doi.org/10.7554/eLife.62852*

2   Albert Einstein College of Medicine. (2022). *The Longevity Genes Project.* https://www.einsteinmed.edu/centers/aging/longevity-genes-project/

3   Chistiakov, D. A., Sobenin, I. A., Revin, V. V., Orekhov, A. N. & Bobryshev, Y. V. (2014). Mitochondrial aging and age-related dysfunction of mitochondria. *Biomed Res Int.* DOI: 10.1155/2014/238463.

4   Sinclair, D. (2019). *Lifespan: Why We Age – and Why We Don't Have To.* HarperCollins. Citing Hubbard, B. P. & Sinclair, D. A. (2014). Small molecule SIRT1 activators for the treatment of aging and age-related diseases, *Trends Pharmacol Sci, 35*(3), 146–54. DOI: 10.1016/j.tips.2013.12.004.

5   Osterloff, E. (n.d.). *Are Lobsters Immortal?, What On Earth*, Natural History Museum. *https://www.nhm.ac.uk/discover/what-on-earth.html*

6   Our cells do not use all of our genes all of the time. They express only those genes that are needed for whatever function is needed at any particular time – for instance, during development, to make a nerve cell different from a kidney cell.

7   Gupta, R. (2018). *The epigenetics of stress.* BioTechniques. *https://www.biotechniques.com/news/the-epigenetics-of-stress/#:~:text=A%20new%20study%20shows%20that,turning%20genes%20on%20or%20off*

8   Bays, B. (2012) *The Journey. An Extraordinary Guide for Healing your Life and Setting Yourself Free.* HarperCollins.

9   Cleveland Clinic. (2022). *Integumentary System. https://my.clevelandclinic.org/health/body/22827-integumentary-system#:~:text=Your%20integumentary%20system%20is%20your,to%20keep%20it%20in%20balance*

10 Environmental Working Group. (2009). *Pollution in People: Cord blood contaminants in minority newborns. https://www.ewg.org/research/pollution-minority-newborns*

11   American Psychological Association. (2023). *Stress effects on the body.* https://www.apa.org/topics/stress/body

12   Global Wellness Institute. (n.d.). *What is wellness?* https://globalwellnessinstitute.org/what-is-wellness/

13   Shimizu, C., Wakita, Y., Inoue, T., Hiramitsu, M., Okada, M., Mitani, Y., Segawa, S., Tsuchiya, Y. & Nabeshima, T. (2019). Effects of lifelong intake of lemon polyphenols on ageing and intestinal microbiome in the senescence-accelerated mouse prone 1 (SAMP1). *Sci Rep,* vol. 9. *https://doi.org/10.1038/s41598-019-40253-x*

14   Kania-Dobrowolska, M. & Baraniak, J. (2022). Dandelion (Taraxacum officinale L.) as a Source of Biologically Active Compounds Supporting the Therapy of Co-Existing Diseases in Metabolic Syndrome. *Foods, vol.*11(18), 2858. DOI: 10.3390/foods11182858.

15   Innes, J. K. & Calder, P. C. (2018). Omega-6 fatty acids and inflammation. *Prostaglandins Leukot Essent Fatty Acids,* 132, 41-48. DOI: 10.1016/j.plefa.2018.03.004.

16   Science Daily. (2014). *Surface area of the digestive tract much smaller than previously thought. https://www.sciencedaily.com/releases/2014/04/140423111505.htm*

17   Tulstrup, M. V., Christensen, E. G., Carvalho, V., Linninge, C., Ahrne, S., Højberg, O., Licht, T. R. & Bahl, M. I. (2021). Antibiotic Treatment Affects Intestinal Permeability and Gut Microbial Composition in Wistar Rats Dependent on Antibiotic Class. *PLoS One,* 10(12). DOI:10.1371/journal.pone.0144854. *See also* Al Dera, H., Alrafaei, B., Tamimi, M., Alfawaz, H. A., Bhat, R. S., Soliman, D. A., Abuaish, S. & El-Ansary, A. (2021). Leaky gut biomarkers in casein- and gluten-rich diet fed rat model of autism. *Translational Neuroscience 12*(1), 601-610. DOI: 10.1515/tnsci-2020-0207.

17b Christovich, A. & Luo, X. M. (2022). Gut Microbiota, Leaky Gut, and Autoimmune Diseases. *Front Immunol 13,* 946248. DOI: 10.3389/fimmu.2022.946248.

18   Fernández-Pérez, S., Pérez-Andrés, J., Gutiérrez, S., Navasa, N., Martínez-Blanco, H., Ferrero, M., A., Vivas, S., Vaquero, L., Iglesias, C., Casqueiro, J. & Rodríguez-Aparicio, L. B. (2020). The human digestive tract is capable of degrading gluten from birth. *Int J Mol Sci, 21*(20), 7696. DOI: *10.3390/ijms21207696.*

19 Goldenberg, J. Z., et al. (2021) Efficacy and safety of low and very low carbohydrate diets for type 2 diabetes remission: systematic review and meta-analysis of published and unpublished randomized trial data. *BMJ, 13*. DOI: 10.1136/bmj.m4743.

20 Knuppel, A., Fensom, G. K., Watts, E. L., Gunter, M. J., Murphy, N., Papier, K., Perez-Cornago, A., Schmidt, J. A., Byrne, K. S., Travis, R. C. & Key, T. J. (2020). Circulating Insulin-like Growth Factor-I Concentrations and Risk of 30 Cancers: Prospective Analyses in UK Biobank. *Cancer Research, 80*(18), 4014–4021. *https://doi. org/10.1158/0008-5472.CAN-20-1281*

21 Harvard T.H. Chan. (2023). *Calcium.* https://www.hsph.harvard. edu/nutritionsource/calcium #:~:text=The%20RDA%20for%20 adults%20is,with%20a%20diagnosis%20of%20osteoporosis.

22 Kanter, J. & Bornfeldt, K. (2016). Impact of Diabetes *Mellitus, Arteriosclerosis, Thrombosis and Vascular Biology, 36*(6), 1049-1053. *https://doi.org/10.1161/ATVBAHA.116.307302*

23 Grizzanti J. et al. (2023). KATP channels are necessary for glucose-dependent increases in amyloid-β and Alzheimer's disease-related pathology. *JCI Insight, 8*(10). doi: 10.1172/jci.insight.162454.

24 Food Standards Agency. (2022). *Acrylamide.* https://www.food.gov. uk/safety-hygiene/acrylamide

25 Bongers, M. L., Hogervorst, J. G., Schouten, L. J., Goldbohm, R. A., Schouten, H. C., van den Brandt, P. A. (2012). Dietary acrylamide intake and the risk of lymphatic malignancies: the Netherlands Cohort Study on diet and cancer. *PLoS One, 7*(6). DOI: 0.1371/ journal.pone.0038016.

26 Markowiak, P. & Slizewska, K. (2017). Effects of Probiotics, Prebiotics, and Synbiotics on Human Health. *Nutrients, 9*(9). DOI: 10.3390/nu9091021.

27 NHS. (2023). *Metabolic syndrome. https://www.nhs.uk/conditions/ metabolic-syndrome/*

28 Rebersek, M. (2021). Gut microbiome and its role in colorectal cancer. *BMC Cancer, 21*, 1325. *https://doi.org/10.1186/ s12885-021-09054-2*

29 Collen. A. (2015). *10% Human, How your body's microbes Hold the key to Health and Happiness.* William Collins.

30 Sinatra, S. T., Sinatra, D. S., Sinatra, S. W. & Chevalier, G. (2022). Grounding – The universal anti-inflammatory remedy. *Biomed*, *46*(1), 11–16. DOI: 10.1016/j.bj.2022.12.002.

31 Warburg O. (1966). *The prime cause and prevention of cancer – Part 1 with two prefaces on prevention.* Available at: http://healingtools. tripod.com/primecause1.html/.

32 National Kidney Foundation. (2024). *Metabolic Acidosis.* https:// www.kidney.org/atoz/content/metabolic-acidosis

33 Caso, G. & Garlick, P. J. (2005). Control of muscle protein kinetics by acid-base balance. *Curr Opin Clin Nutr Metab Care, 8*(1), 73-6. DOI: 10.1097/00075197-200501000-00011.

34 Ahmad, A. S., Ormiston-Smith, N. & Sasieni, P. D. (2015). Trends in the lifetime risk of developing cancer in Great Britain: comparison of risk for those born from 1930 to 1960. *Br J Cancer, 112*(5), 943-947. DOI: 10.1038/bjc.2014.606.

35 Anand, P., et al. (2008). Cancer is a preventable disease that requires major lifestyle changes. *Pharm Res, 25*(9), 2097-116. DOI: 10.1007/ s11095-008-9661-9.

36 World Health Organization. (2020). *The top 10 causes of death.* https://www.who.int/news-room/fact-sheets/detail/ the-top-10-causes-of-death

37 Cancer Research UK. (n.d.). *Cancer incidence by age.* https:// www.cancerresearchuk.org/health-professional/cancer-statistics/ incidence/age?

38 Hanahan D & Weinberg R. A. (2000). The hallmarks of cancer. *Cell, 100*(1):57-70. doi:10.1016/s0092-8674(00)81683-9. PMID: 10647931.

39 Kiechle. M, et al. (2016). Effects of lifestyle intervention in BRCA1/2 mutation carriers on nutrition, BMI, and physical fitness (LIBRE study): study protocol for a randomized controlled trial. *Trials. 17*, 368. DOI: 10.1186/s13063-016-1504-0.

40 Gebremedhin, T. K., Cherie, A., Tolera, B. D., Atinafu, B. T. & Demelew, T. M. (2021). Prevalence and risk factors of malnutrition among adult cancer patients receiving chemotherapy treatment

41 Campbell II, T. M. (2004). *The China study: the most comprehensive study of nutrition ever conducted and the startling implications for diet, weight loss and long-term health.* BenBella Books, Inc.

42 Muscaritoli, M., et al. (2021). ESPEN practical guideline: Clinical Nutrition in cancer. *Clin Nutr, 40*(5), 2898–2913. DOI: 10.1016/j. clnu.2021.02.005.

43 Gangadharan, A., et al. (2017). Protein calorie malnutrition, nutritional intervention and personalized cancer care. *Oncotarget, 8*(14), 24009-24030. DOI: 10.18632/oncotarget.15103.

44 World Health Organization. (2002). *Protein and Amino Acid Requirements in Human Nutrition: report of a joint FAO/WHO/UNU expert consultation. https://apps.who.int/iris/handle/10665/43411*

45 Halton, T. L. & Hu, F. B. (2004). The effects of high protein diets on thermogenesis, satiety and weight loss: a critical review. *Journal of the American College of Nutrition, 23*(5):373-85. DOI: 10.1080/07315 724.2004.10719381.

46 Sandoval-Insausti, H., Chiu, Y., Wang, Y., Hart, J., Bhupathiraju, S. N., Mínguez-Alarcón, L., Ding, M., Willett, W. C., Laden, F. & Chavarro, J. E. (2022). Intake of fruits and vegetables according to pesticide residue status in relation to all-cause and disease-specific mortality: Results from three prospective cohort studies. *Environ Int, 15*, 159:107024. DOI: 10.1016/j.envint.2021.107024.

47 Chiu, Y. H., et al. (2018). EARTH Study Team. Association Between Pesticide Residue Intake From Consumption of Fruits and Vegetables and Pregnancy Outcomes Among Women Undergoing Infertility Treatment With Assisted Reproductive Technology. *JAMA Intern Med, 178*(1), 17-26. doi: 10.1001/jamainternmed.2017.5038.

48 Falconer, I. R. (2006). Are endocrine disrupting compounds a health risk in drinking water?. *Int J Environ Res Public Health, 3*(2), 180-184. DOI: 10.3390/ijerph2006030020.

49 Maia, E. W., et al. (2021). Cruciferous vegetable consumption and pancreatic cancer: A case-control study, *Cancer Epidemiology, 72*. https://doi.org/10.1016/j.canep.2021.101924.

50 Verhoeven, D. T., Goldbohm, R. A., van Poppel, G., Verhagen, H. & van den Brandt, P. A. (2006). Epidemiological studies on brassica vegetables and cancer risk. *Cancer Epidemiol Biomarkers Prev., 5*(9), 733-48. *Epidemiological studies on brassica vegetables and cancer risk - PubMed (nih.gov)*

51 Pierce, J., Natarajan, L., Newman, V., Barbier, L., Mohler, J., Rock, C., Heath, D., Guru, K., Jameson, M., Li, H., Mirheydar, H., Holmes, M. & Marshall, J. (2013). A Randomized Pilot Trial of Dietary Modification for the Chemoprevention of Noninvasive Bladder Cancer: The Dietary Intervention in Bladder Cancer Study. *Cancer Prev Res (Phila), 6*(9), 971–978. DOI: 10.1158/1940-6207. CAPR-13-0050.

52 Lam, T. K, et al. (2009). Cruciferous vegetable consumption and lung cancer risk: a systematic review. *Cancer Epidemiol Biomarkers Prev, 18*(1), 184-95. DOI: 10.1158/1055-9965.EPI-08-0710.

53 Gabor M. (2003). *When the Body Says No: The Cost of Hidden Stress.* Vintage Canada.

54 Hannibal, K. E. & Bishop, M. D. (2014). Chronic stress, cortisol dysfunction, and pain: a psychoneuroendocrine rationale for stress management in pain rehabilitation. *Phys Ther, 94*(12), 1816-25. DOI:10.2522/ptj.20130597.

55 Salleh, M. R. (2008). Life event, stress and illness. *Malays J Med Sci, 15*(4):9-18. *https://www.ncbi.nlm.nih.gov/pmc/articles/PMC3341916/*

56 Weil. (n.d.). *Breathing Exercises www.drweil.com/videos-features/ videos/breathing-exercises-4-7-8-breath/*

57 Stapleton, P., Crighton, G., Sabot, D. & O'Neill, H. M. (2020). Reexamining the effect of emotional freedom techniques on stress biochemistry: A randomized controlled trial. *Psychol Trauma, 12*(8), 869-877. DOI: 10.1037/tra0000563.

58 Gosain, R., Gage-Bouchard, E., Ambrosone, C., Repasky, E. & Gandhi, S. (2020). Stress reduction strategies in breast cancer: review of pharmacologic and non-pharmacologic based strategies. *Semin Immunopathol, 42*(6), 719-734. DOI: 10.1007/s00281-020-00815-y.

59 Roehrs, T. & Roth, T. (2001). Sleep, Sleepiness, and Alcohol Use. *Alcohol Research and Health, 25*(2), 101-109. *https://pubmed.ncbi. nlm.nih.gov/11584549/*

60 Metta Institute. (2011). *Metta Meditation. https://www. mettainstitute.org/mettameditation.html*

61 Verheul, H. M & Pinedo, H. M. (2000). The role of vascular endothelial growth factor (VEGF) in tumor angiogenesis and early clinical development of VEGF-receptor kinase inhibitors. *Clinical Breast Cancer.* DOI: 10.3816/cbc.2000.s.015.

62 Waziry, R., Ryan, C.P., Corcoran, D.L. et al. Effect of long-term caloric restriction on DNA methylation measures of biological aging in healthy adults from the CALERIE trial. Nat Aging 3, 248–257 (2023). https://doi.org/10.1038/s43587-022-00357-y

63 Shanmugalingam, T., Bosco, C., Ridley, A. J. & Van Hemelrijck, M. (2016). Is there a role for IGF-1 in the development of second primary cancers?. *Cancer Med, 5*(11), 3353-3367. DOI: 10.1002/cam4.871.

64 Chan, S. & Debono, M. (2010). Replication of cortisol circadian rhythm: new advances in hydrocortisone replacement therapy. *Ther Adv Endocrinol Metab, 1*(3), 129–138. DOI: 10.1177/2042018810380214

65 Nencioni, A., Caffa, I., Cortellino, S. & Longo, Valter D. (2018). Fasting and cancer: molecular mechanisms and clinical application. *Nature Reviews: Cancer, 18*(11), 707–719. DOI: 10.1038/s41568-018-0061-0

66 Prof. Valter Longo. (2019). *Fasting Mimicking Program & Longevity. https://www.valterlongo.com/fasting-mimicking-program-and-longevity/*

67 Butt, M. S. & Sultan, M. T. (2009). Green tea: nature's defense against malignancies. *Crit Rev Food Sci Nutr, 49*(5), 463-73. DOI: 10.1080/10408390802145310. PMID: 19399671.

68 Ganesan, K., Xu, B. (2017). Polyphenol-Rich Lentils and Their Health Promoting Effects. *Int J Mol Sci, 18*(11), 2390. DOI: 10.3390/ijms18112390.

69 Ba, Djibril, M. et al. (year). Higher Mushroom Consumption Is Associated with Lower Risk of Cancer: A Systematic Review and Meta-Analysis of Observational Studies. *Advances in Nutrition, 12*(5),1691–1704. DOI: 10.1093/advances/nmab015.

70 Rosendahl, A. H., Sun, C., Wu, D. & Andersson, R. (2012). Polysaccharide-K (PSK) increases p21(WAF/Cip1) and promotes apoptosis in pancreatic cancer cells. *Pancreatology, 12*(6), 467-474. DOI: 10.1016/j.pan.2012.09.004.

71 Warburton, D. E., Nicol, C. W. & Bredin, S. S. (2006). Health benefits of physical activity: the evidence. *CMAJ, 174*(6), 801-9. DOI: 10.1503/cmaj.051351.

72 Gerhart-Hines, Z., et al. (2011). The cAMP/PKA pathway rapidly activates SIRT1 to promote fatty acid oxidationindependently of changes in NAD(+). *Mol Cell, 44*(6), 851-63. DOI: 10.1016/j.molcel.2011.12.005.

73 Ferraresi, C, Huang, Y. Y. & Hamblin, M. R. (2016). Photobiomodulation in human muscle tissue: an advantage in sports performance?' *J Biophotonics, 9*(11-12), 1273–1299. DOI: 10.1002/jbio.201600176.

74 Wunsch, A. & Matuschka, K. (2014). A controlled trial to determine the efficacy of red and near-infrared light treatment in patient satisfaction, reduction of fine lines, wrinkles, skin roughness, and intradermal collagen density increase. *Photomed Laser Surg, 32*(2), 93–100. DOI: 10.1089/pho.2013.3616.

75 The benefits of essiac have not been scientifically investigated; however, the individual ingredients have been shown to support kidney health (burdock root) and gut lining (slippery elm), stimulate gut movement and water into intestines to hasten excretion of waste (sheep sorrel) and have anti-inflammatory and anti-cancer effects (Indian rhubarb root).

One final note

Dear Reader,

It would be great to hear from you.

If you want to share anything that has lead you to this book and if you need further support please send me a note at:

bridget@bridgetlouisenutrition.com

Wishing you a long and healthy life

Bridget

Lobsters can regenerate limbs, with claw regeneration taking up to 5 years. Similarly, humans can regenerate liver and lung tissues, potentially extending lifespan. Lobsters regenerate vital tools for obtaining food, notably the 2 front limbs, where one is for crushing and the other is used for cutting.